"Tara Leigh Cobble does in print what she's always managed to do so well in life ... she simply is who she is, and we get to see God between every single line."

—BEBO NORMAN, *recording artist*

"Tara Leigh's journey—whether from venue to venue or through each season of her life—passes through loneliness and heartache and uncertainty. But instead of lingering there, she keeps barreling toward her final destination: grace. Ride shotgun with her for a few miles, and she'll take you there, too."

—JASON BOYETT, *author of*
Pocket Guide to the Bible

"If your soul is in need of some fresh air, this book is a great place to take a deep breath!"

—JOE BATLUCK, *pastor to students,*
Denton Bible Church, Denton, Texas

"Tara Leigh Cobble shares her journey into adulthood with a poignant honesty that will shake you up, make you laugh, warm your heart ... and leave you wanting more."

—JOANNA HARRIS ILLINGWORTH,
author of You Didn't Complete Me

"Everyone will identify with this book on some level; we all have a story and are playing a role in a much bigger story than our own. Tara Leigh has the guts to lay it all out for better or worse, which is quite admirable in my book."

—TODD BRAGG, *drummer for Caedmon's Call*

"Open-hearted, determinedly intelligent, quirky, and, above all, honest, *Here's to Hindsight* is a treat for the entire spectrum of mind, soul, and spirit, giving the reader an endlessly engaging glimpse at the impact of a personal journey with Christ."

—KEMPER CRABB, *musician and theologian*

"Tara Leigh is kind enough to let me learn from her stories without walking away with her scars. Her Jedi-like ability to sneak in amazing life lessons while she amuses with her experiences not only makes it a fun, easy, and interesting read, but one that leaves a mark too."

—DAVE BARNES, *singer/songwriter*

"In *Here's to Hindsight*, Tara Leigh Cobble cordially opens the passenger door to her Toyota Camry and invites you to hop in for the ride of her life. Tara Leigh's abundant and hard-earned knowledge is not only invaluable to the independent music artist, but to all twentysomethings who are looking to make sense of how God is shaping their story."

—JOSH WILSON, *recording artist*

"If Donald Miller were a pretty girl from East Tennessee, his name might be Tara Leigh Cobble. With grace, quirkiness, and maturity, Cobble shares her raw, intimate, and sometimes clumsy story of learning how God threads Himself into a journey. *Here's to Hindsight* will help you see that thread in your own story."

—MATTHEW PAUL TURNER, *author of* Mind Games

Here's to Hindsight

letters to my former self

TARA LEIGH COBBLE

[RELEVANTBOOKS]

Published by RELEVANT Books
A division of RELEVANT Media Group, Inc.

www.relevantbooks.com
www.relevantmediagroup.com

© 2006 RELEVANT Media Group

Design by RELEVANT Solutions
Cover design by Anna Melcon, Jeremy Kennedy
Interior design by Anna Melcon, Jen Revoltar

RELEVANT Books is a registered trademark of RELEVANT Media
Group, Inc., and is registered in the U.S. Patent and Trademark Office.

Library of Congress Control Number: 2006904069
International Standard Book Number: 0-9768175-9-4

For information or bulk orders:
RELEVANT MEDIA GROUP, INC.
100 SOUTH LAKE DESTINY DR., STE. 200
ORLANDO, FL 32810
407-660-1411

06 07 08 09 10 8 7 6 5 4 3 2 1

Printed in the United States of America

This book is dedicated to my parents, who first taught me to pay attention to the details of the story that God is writing in all of our lives.

Contents

Acknowledgments

I'd like to acknowledge the following people for their help in making this story come alive, do cartwheels, eat a burrito, and then take a nap on the beach.

Beth Polkinghorn, who patiently guided me through style lessons and who read this book more times than I have. Thanks for being my friend, my tutor, and a fellow fan of the Oxford comma.

Micha Boyett Hohorst, my favorite writer of all time, who taught me everything I know about memoir writing and who reminded me that God gives each of us a story to tell.

Cameron, Cara, Tia, Susan, Betsy, and the rest of the RELEVANT crew, who believed in me and supported me throughout this process.

My other insightful friends who walked through this process with me: Jason Boyett, Jane Choe, Kemper Crabb, Anne Carpenter, Matt Lehman, Joshua Blankenship, John Varghese, Ryan Greenawalt, Carla Jean (is-not-my-lover) Whitley, Kris Swiatocho, Basim Nasr, Mike Hon, and Ester Bloom and all the Wednesday Writers: Michael, Marsha, and Sharon.

Those of you who have been kind enough to let me include you in my story: my gracious family, Pretend-I'm-Not-Asian Jane, Danger, Judy Scheuch, Hot Nathan, Christine, Sarcastic Paul, Meredith, Kelly, Amber & Matt, Shannon & Jeremy, Jenny, Katie, Emily O., Stephanie, Josh Wilson, Antonio, Harry, Lacey, Rainey, Scott, Tom, Emily, Brooke & Ashley, Ricky Jackson, Mrs. Clara King, Dr. Evans, Elisabeth Elliot, Donald Miller, Kirk Cameron, Evel Knievel, Kierstin Berry, Lauren F. Winner, Debbie Lollis, Seth Whalen, Grassroots Music, Matt, Jackson, Todd, Andy Beard, Tamara, John Delony, Eric & Danielle Peters, Sam, Brad, Susan, Alan, Stephen, Dan, Bobby, Vickie, Damon, Marge, Derek Webb, Cliff Young, Bill Hemmer, David Letterman, Johnny Carson, Jon Stewart, Conan O'Brien, and the writers of the songs that have been my personal soundtrack.

For the creative environments: Fido, where I wrote most of this book and made so many new friends along the way (special thanks to Joshua, my favorite barista), Frothy Monkey, Bongo Java, Café Coco, Café Ari, Janice Tilley's house, Boo & Deke Andrews' house (Shiloh), and hotel rooms across America.

Introduction

If I were interested in making things up instead of being honest, this book would've opened with the sentence: "So far, my life has been filled with ice cream and attractive suitors." Instead, it opens with a statement that has far more truth to it: "My parents did not raise me to be like this."

However, I do want to protect the identities of certain people in the story, so some things in this book have been altered slightly for various reasons. Defining characteristics, locations, and appearances may have been altered.

I've also made some slight changes for the sake of simplifying. All of my road managers have been condensed into the person I refer to as "Susan." Two of them actually were named Susan, so most of the time the road manager you're reading about really is Susan.

The stories themselves are as real as I can remember them, except when I remembered them but had to condense the time frame in order to prevent the story from dragging on endlessly and forcing you into a coma. The quotes are as close as possible to the real thing, but since I don't carry a tape recorder with me everywhere I go, they're bound to be off a bit somewhere. In general, this is the way things went as best as I can recall them.

There's still a lot of learning and growing for me to do. I'll probably look back on this book years from now and cringe over how wrong I was about certain things. So don't necessarily put a lot of stock in what I've said unless you find that it measures up to the Truth—in which case, put stock in the Truth, not in me.

All of these things are a part of the story of God's handiwork in my life and how I've seen it unfold. He has used it to teach me how to love Him and follow Him better. Hopefully it will be something you can relate to—broken pieces and unexpected discoveries and all.

Fundamentalism & Misdemeanors

MY PARENTS DID NOT RAISE ME TO BE LIKE THIS,
I thought as I typed in my address and a fake name.

That was probably the fifteenth time I had put down phony
information on the forms and sent them off, so you'd think I would
have been immune to any tugs on my conscience. I wheeled my
chair out from under my desk, looked around the corner to make
sure my boss wasn't watching me, and then hit "Send."

I didn't fear losing my job, which was straight out of *Office
Space*—the kind of job that grates on your soul, little by little,
until you are ready to beat yourself in the head with the three-hole
punch—but I've always hated the thought of getting in trouble for
anything.

At the time, I was juggling fifteen hours of college courses
while working fifty-hour weeks at the furniture company, and the
job didn't pay jack, which only made me loathe it more. Every day

while I sat at my desk, I burned with jealousy when I thought of all my friends who had moved off to big cities to attend college. But through a series of unanticipated events, I was stuck in Greeneville, Tennessee, my tiny hometown (population: 14,000) in the foothills of the Appalachian Mountains.

My parents had initially suggested that I attend a strict Christian college in upstate New York. But when we went to visit, the campus reminded me of the setting of the Friday the 13th movies, so I'm glad they were cool enough to let me make my own decision about what school to attend. And frankly, my notion of an ideal college experience never included the words *curfew*, *demerits*, or *chaperoned coed outings*.

I preferred words like *Wall*, *Street*, and *Journal*, or anything else business-oriented. My fascination with reading *The Wall Street Journal* started shortly after I transferred to public school in sixth grade. Years of private Christian schooling had put me so far ahead of the rest of the students that I didn't learn anything in public school for the first three years. Nerd city. My teachers, being the creatively cruel beings that they were, thought my lack of popularity needed to be emphasized a bit more, so they sent me to be tested for the gifted class. When I met the criteria, they immediately shuffled me in, happy to be rid of the smart-aleck kid who thought she knew all the answers.

In the sixth-grade gifted class, we studied finance and the stock market. We subscribed to *The Wall Street Journal* and "bought" stocks, which we tracked throughout the course of the year. I made nearly $70,000 in fake money when my stocks tripled. What they say about rich people being able to buy friends isn't true—at least for *fake* rich people—because no one wanted to be my friend even though I was clearly loaded.

During the second semester, Brooke York and Ashley Madison began talking to me. I suspected they were trying to steal stock tips, because they had never spoken to me before. *Could this be my chance to break out of my stiff reputation as the prudish girl from the private Christian school and into the cool crowd? Maybe they'll even ask me to go to the mall with them!*

Brooke and Ashley were The Popular Girls—leggy blondes who were wealthy and intelligent, as if God had used all of His bonus options on them. I was mousy and plain and deeply obsessed with Alex P. Keaton—so when they dubbed me "Miss Perfect," I took it as a compliment instead of the insult they intended.

I had been a big fish in a small pond in private school. But public school was a brand-new environment where I was desperate for an identity, and that moniker seemed more favorable than the other nickname I had acquired: "Holy Roller." So I owned it. I wanted to live up to "Miss Perfect," because I guess I thought that if they were jealous of my brain, then at least I had *that* going for me—I had something they wanted, something that made me feel valuable.

* * *

Throughout middle school and high school, I studied like a fiend. During my sophomore year, I decided to graduate a year early so I could get out of Greeneville and into Harvard as quickly as possible (assuming—quite presumptuously—that I would get in). By junior year, I had time for little more than studying, which usually amounted to six or seven hours each night. The straps on my backpack broke twice that year from the weight of all the books I carried around. You can imagine how popular I became with the boys. They just love a bookish girl. I felt certain I would've been crowned Homecoming Queen—*if all the other girls in school had spontaneously combusted.*

Then it happened: halfway through spring semester, I burned out. I had been taking a lot of extra classes that year so that I could graduate early, and academia suddenly became oppressive. My burnout was so severe that I even stopped watching *Jeopardy*. My parents noted my struggle and suggested that I stick around for my senior year. I wholeheartedly agreed. I took a load of electives like photography and journalism so that I could coast for a while before graduating with my class.

During my senior year, my grandfather passed away, and my family inherited a house to maintain, so I was given the option of moving into it on my own and renting it from my family. This seemed like a better option than living in a cramped dorm room with a potentially psychotic stranger and eating ramen for four years, so I opted to stay in Greeneville. And frankly, I was lingering a bit too long in that burned-out, lazy state of mind. Had I been at Harvard when my grandfather died, I probably would not have moved back home to live in his house. But as it was, it felt like my reasons to go to college nearby outweighed my reasons to leave.

* * *

The imaginary descent from Harvard undergrad to miserable office worker at a furniture company haunted me. *Where did my life go? Why didn't I graduate in three years like I'd planned?* Then I wouldn't be stuck in Greeneville in the death grip of this job. I spent hours answering complaint calls from customers, sending out replacement products, telling people how to assemble their lovely new desks and entertainment centers, and secretly plotting to burn the place down with one flash of my eye, as soon as I learned how to tap into that specific superpower.

Perhaps it was the boredom that led me to falsify information on the forms. Or perhaps it was my disdain for my boss, who spewed Christian rhetoric while having an affair. I wanted so much to tell my coworkers that this man did *not* represent the Christian faith at large. Meanwhile, I was stealing from the company.

Not in actual dollars, mind you. And not in any real way that hurt them, but it was stealing nonetheless. And I was crafty in my approach, which gave me a sense of pride in my "work."

Every year the company discontinued a line of furniture, and all the leftover parts and pieces sat in the warehouse, unused. The only time those parts saw the light of day was if a customer purchased a piece of furniture on clearance and it was missing a part. Then they would call my customer service line. I would make note of what they were missing, send out an order to retrieve it from the warehouse, and ship it to them free of charge.

One day I received a call from a customer who complained that he was missing nearly everything. "It seems like all this guy purchased was an empty box with our phone number on it!" I complained to a coworker while covering the mouthpiece with my hand. "Do I send him *all* this stuff?"

"That's the arrangement," she said in a voice that conveyed our mutual bewilderment.

That's when I launched my plan to steal a discontinued entertainment center, piece by piece. I did it over the course of a year, secretly mailing myself boards and screws and glass doors. I even sent myself *extra* parts, in case I ever accidentally shattered one of the glass doors.

I shipped them at random intervals, using assumed names. After a while, I started getting clever with the false identities. I sent a chrome leg to "David L. Etterman" and another to "John E.

Carson" on the same day. I stopped just short of the late-night TV hosts hat trick—I saved "Conan O. Brien" for the following week.

I stored the parts in my basement until I had them all, and then assembled my beautiful entertainment center one day after class. It was sleek and black with chrome accents and double glass doors to cover the DVD and VCR racks. My friends were all jealous of it. And every time I looked at it, it made me sick.

But eventually, I got over that. The callousness came gradually but surely. I had been tossing my standards and beliefs aside for quite some time, and I was pretty good at it by that point.

Chutes & Ladders

I'VE NEVER BEEN A BIG QUESTIONER of the facts
associated with my faith. I used to feel guilty about that, as though
it would validate my beliefs more if I had experienced doubt.
Besides, all the cool kids had gone through their doubting phases,
where they read Nietzsche and said things to our Sunday school
teacher like, "But isn't it circular reasoning to believe that the
Bible is true only because it says in the Bible that it is true?" This
is not to say that I've been spoon-fed; it's just that I wasn't only
told *what* to believe, but I was also taught *why* it was true. My
parents were bent on exploring apologetics and hermeneutics with
us at home. They essentially nipped my doubt in the bud.

When I was in middle school, my dad and I spent nearly a
month reading through all the references to angels in the Bible.
We used his gigantic copy of *Strong's Exhaustive Concordance
of the Bible* and looked up all 315 corresponding verses in the

King James Version. The point of this, he said, was to compare
the Bible's description of angels to the modern-day interpretation
of angels. "There isn't really anything in the Bible that points to
angels having two wings or halos, like we see in all the paintings
and statues," he told me. "And messenger angels, the kind that
appeared to people in the Bible, were always men. They never
showed up as women or with wings."

And he was right. The only time we found anything about
wings was on cherubim and seraphim, and seraphim had six wings,
not two—a pair to cover their feet, a pair to cover their faces, and
a pair to fly. These are the kinds of things my dad taught me; he
wanted me to excavate the pieces of my faith so that I could grasp
the truth. So you can imagine that if he spent that much time on
angels, he would've spent far more time on things like grace and
faith. And he did.

I've learned and grown so much from the things I was taught in
the blank white walls of a strict Christian academy and in the pews
of an independent, fundamental Baptist church. But I've also challenged (and changed) many of the beliefs I grew up with.

The school we attended was very small, despite the fact that
it encompassed all grades. Things that were pretty much unac-
ceptable there included shorts, pants (for women), dancing, or
any mention of going to the movies. When I switched to public
school, I was shocked to find out that some of the kids had cable
television because, according to my former teachers at the private
school, cable television was "nothing but filth." I honestly thought
that HBO stood for "Hell's Box Office" until I saw an ad for it on
television when I was twelve.

That was long before girls went wild and spring break became a
weeklong orgy broadcast on MTV. Comparatively, those were days

of innocence and purity on television, but I had come to believe that television was the devil's playground. That's a heavy thought for an eleven-year-old to carry.

As I became surrounded by all kinds of things that contradicted my early training, I was confused. *Doesn't everyone who drinks become an alcoholic? Doesn't everyone who dances engage in premarital sex?*

I watched some of my siblings rebel against the things we'd been taught in that Christian school, but I didn't want to push my parents' buttons that way. Or maybe I also believed that some of it really was true and worthwhile. I kept trying to find the balance.

I'm a big fan of being right, of having a complete grip on the answers. Even if I don't live out the truth, I still like to know what it is. This is probably a pride issue. Every step along my journey of faith, I was sure that I had reached the full revelation of the truth, but then I'd take a step in a different direction and think, *Okay, now I have a full understanding of things.* Then it would change again. I'm so full of it sometimes.

But the one thing that remained was this: I never questioned if God existed or if He cared. I knew that the Bible was true, that Jesus had died on the cross for my sins. I never questioned if Jesus loved me. The thing I questioned was if I was going to love Him back. *He loves me, but is it worth the supposed sacrifices I'll have to make to follow Him? He loves me, but would I rather ignore that and do my own thing?*

For a while, I wasn't really sure how to start answering that question.

* * *

My earliest memory is probably from age three, of the time when
my mom taught me John 3:16 while I played with Lincoln Logs
at the foot of her sewing machine. My family didn't have a lot of
money back then, especially with six kids, who were all in ex-
pensive, private Christian schools. I have no idea how my parents
made ends meet. It probably had something to do with the fact that
we had timed showers, measured baths, and "only three ice cubes
per cup, because ice costs money, you know."

My dad worked at his bookstore six days a week; my mom
spent her days giving perms and cuts in her beauty salon, and her
nights sewing clothes for us. Every night, I played at her feet with
a toy and my blanket. She talked to me about Jesus, recited verses,
and sang to me until I fell asleep. Sometimes I woke up later as my
dad carried me to bed while humming one of the hymns she'd been
singing. I liked those times the best, because I could see, through
sleepy eyes, the way they loved me so tenderly.

I idolized each of my siblings. I'm the youngest of the six
(three boys and three girls), so as the Cindy Brady of the family,
I tried hard to walk in their shadows as precisely as possible. I
wanted to be as studious as Jeff, as charming as Gina, as kind as
Sonya, as helpful as Jon, and as funny as Jason. Since Jason was
closest in age to me—six years older—I spent the majority of my
time with him. I noticed that everyone loved him—specifically,
everyone I admired. And as they all laughed at his wit, I stood by,
taking notes and stealing his jokes. I seized every possible opportunity to be near him.

One Saturday night when I was about four years old, Jason and
I were in our pajamas playing Chutes and Ladders while my mom
folded laundry in the next room. I don't remember exactly how it
happened, but he asked me if I wanted to be a Christian. I said I

did, and we prayed and asked Jesus to forgive my sins and be my Lord. Just like that.

The next morning, my dad, who was the head deacon at our church, shared the news with the congregation. After church, my family celebrated over lunch, and we were allowed to drink Coke that day because it was a "special occasion." I remember my dad quizzing me the way parents sometimes do with their kids.

"So tell me ..." he said, leaning in closer and smiling. "Who saved you?"

"Jason did!" I said.

And they all laughed.

"Well, yes, Jason led you to Christ, but *Jesus* is the One who saved you," he said.

"Oh, yeah. That's what I meant."

That night at church (we went to church three times a week: Sunday morning, Sunday night, and Wednesday night), we talked to the pastor about baptizing me. He immersed me the next Sunday morning in the baptismal behind the pulpit, underneath the big wooden cross on the wall. My first symbolic act of my new faith, and I was only four years old. I really don't remember what it's like *not* to know Jesus. Sometimes I'm jealous of the stories of people who have come to know Jesus after years of drug addiction or a life of crime; other times I'm grateful to have such a simple story of my own.

* * *

Blind these eyes who never tried to lose temptation.
—JENNIFER KNAPP, "The Way I Am"

The first time I ever got in trouble was in first grade. I gave math answers to Ricky Jackson, who sat in front of me. I scrawled "4 + 3 = 7" on a piece of paper and slipped it over his left shoulder. I probably helped him cheat because I had a crush on him, and I thought that would make him like me. I had always had crushes on boys, but I often made poor choices about the objects of my affection. Ricky was a bad choice for two reasons: he apparently was not very smart, *and* he was a tattletale.

He raised his hand and whined, "She gave me the answers! She gave me the answers!"

Mrs. King called me to the back of the room, where she wrote a note to my parents at her desk. She told me that she was writing the note in cursive so I couldn't read it, and then she folded it up and put Scotch tape on each edge of her pale pink stationery of death.

But I was already a master of cursive, so I decided to read the note that afternoon while my oldest brother Jeff drove us home. Jeff is eighteen years older than me, and he taught biology at the academy we attended. He drove us to and from school every day in his bright blue Toyota station wagon. That afternoon I sat in the back seat between my other brothers, and I nervously peeled the tape off the edges to read of my impending doom: Mrs. King was going to send me to the principal's office the next morning, where I would get three lashes.

My brothers feigned fear, and their eyes grew big as they warned me about Dr. Evans' "Board of Education"—a long wooden paddle with holes drilled through it. They had all gone through that ordeal before and somehow survived, but I was the first female Cobble to meet the principal's wrath.

By the time we got home, I was sufficiently terrified. I ran into my room, threw myself onto the bed, hid the note under my flowered pillow, and cried myself to sleep. When my parents got home,

Jeff told them the news. They called me into the living room, where my dad was sitting, straight-faced, on the brown couch, and my mom was across from him in her wooden rocking chair. I was too nervous to sit, so I stood between the two of them.

"Do you have something you want to tell us?" my dad asked.

I got choked up when I started to speak, but I managed to say, "I cheated in Mrs. King's class, and they're going to spank me tomorrow. But don't worry—I already asked Jesus to save me again."

That was the night that I came to understand what salvation meant.

My dad pulled me up onto his lap and wiped my eyes with his sleeve. Tenderness and compassion radiated from him as he tucked my bangs behind my ears and smiled at me. He said, "Don't you know that you only have to ask Him to save you once? You don't get kicked out of heaven every time you sin."

He and Mom told me, in words that a child could understand, about what Romans 11 says—that we are saved by God's grace and not by being sinless, because if we were saved by our good actions, then it wouldn't be by His grace. Even my *best* qualities couldn't get me into heaven, Dad said, because they are like dirty rags—but Jesus had saved me anyway, despite all that. He talked a lot about the cross. Somehow, I got it.

At the time, all I could think about was the Board of Education, looming ahead of me like a ticking time bomb. But ultimately, what my parents said to me that night was the most important lesson I've ever learned.

* * *

As a ten-year-old girl with an overactive imagination, I knew that someday—if I played my cards right—I would become Mrs. Kirk Cameron. Thus, I spent some of my allowance on a *Tiger Beat* magazine with him on the cover. When my dad discovered it, he burned it. He didn't want me lusting after or idolizing anyone. In our home, there was no mention of sex—except to say that we shouldn't do it. In fact, when we watched television as a family, Dad would turn it off if two people kissed who weren't married *in real life.*

No *Laverne & Shirley* (they worked in a brewery). No *Happy Days* (Fonzie was a slut). No *Grease* (don't even get me started). My brother Jon joked that we probably shouldn't even dare watch Disney movies, because as soon as Dad walked into the room, Bambi was guaranteed to let out a string of expletives or visit an animated strip club. It was a rigid environment to grow up in, but I didn't really mind. In fact, I hardly noticed until I spent the night at friends' houses and witnessed the alternative.

Though in some ways I was sheltered to an extent that might seem ludicrous, I cannot conceive of a better heritage than the one my parents gave me. They always walked with Christ in a way that showed us how much they loved Him and were devoted to Him. Dad read his Bible every night, led us in Bible study at six o'clock every morning around the kitchen table, and always pulled into the full-service pump at the gas station so that he could have five minutes with the attendant to tell him about Jesus. At the time, it was kind of embarrassing. "Oh no, Dad's witnessing again," we'd say to each other as he pulled out a Jack Chick tract from the front pocket of his short-sleeved button-up shirt and handed it to whatever person he'd just met.

We rode to church in our big brown van every Sunday morning, and I usually wound up sitting on the lap of one of my siblings, because the van was full of all the people Dad had led to Christ and invited to church that week. Sometimes we had to leave almost two hours early to pick up all the people. Anyone walking down the street on our way to church was likely to be invited to hop in, too. On rare occasions, someone would actually join us, this weird group of strangers in a clunky, brown van.

In addition to that, my mom has the gift of incredible, unwavering kindness and hospitality. I have never seen such selfless love. She *lived* the Gospel to everyone in her path. Making gifts for the people at the nursing home, planting flowers outside the windows of bedridden neighbors, feeding a small army of my friends at the drop of a hat, and doing it all without breaking down—I have always been in awe of her.

My parents never cursed, never drank, never went to the movies, never danced—and they implored us to do the same. I'm hesitant to describe it as "legalism" though, because they were careful to teach us that they did these things *because* they love Jesus, not in order to win His love and approval. That's a crucial distinction.

Of all the things they gave me, I am most thankful to my parents for instilling in me an understanding of what it looks like to be above reproach. I sin far more than they would ever imagine, but I still believe what my dad used to say: it's better to do the certain good than the potential evil. I don't despise their strictness, and I was never tempted much to rebel directly against it, although I pushed the boundaries in less obvious ways.

3

Pebble in My Shoe

THE WEEK AFTER HIGH-SCHOOL GRADUATION, I
moved into my late grandfather's old, empty house. My Christian
community disappeared as my friends went off to college, and I
began to scrape around trying to find a new group of friends. I did
not know it at the time, but this move would send me spiraling into
the darkest period of my life. I didn't make wise choices about
those new friends—I doled out my friendship on a "first come, first
served" basis.

Lacey, whom I affectionately referred to as Crazy Lacey, was
my best friend. We met one night at a café, where she was on a
first date with a guy I had a crush on. Being very much a girl, I
introduced myself to her just to get the scoop on the situation,
which I soon found out was not promising. Their relationship never
developed, and my crush on him fizzled, but my friendship with
her became a fixture in my life.

For the first six months after I moved out, my dad came over every Sunday morning to make sure I was going to church, since I went to a different church than my parents did. I pretended to be getting up and getting ready, but I wasn't going to church.

I was staying out late on Saturday night with Lacey and my new friends from school and sleeping until noon on Sunday. I was following her lead, kissing boys I barely knew in dorm rooms filled with marijuana smoke and empty Heineken cans. And while I never smoked or drank, I still had to work overtime to ignore the pangs of conscience that crept into my heart. After some practice at pushing conviction aside, I was able to enjoy every minute that I spent on the wrong side of the tracks. "Flirting with sin" is what my dad would've called it.

Lacey was working on her teaching degree, but when she wasn't in school or student-teaching for a kindergarten class, we hung out at her incredibly hip apartment—at the only modern apartment complex in Greeneville—which she decorated with a great collection of furniture and a knack for style more European than Tennessean. I thought she was the coolest person I'd ever met.

* * *

One day, Lacey asked me to take her to get a new tattoo in Asheville, an hour away. "I don't think I'll be able to drive home," she said, "because I'm getting the tattoo on my foot, around my ankle, and up to my calf. It's going to be freaking huge, and it might hurt to push the gas pedal if I had to drive home." What I didn't know at the time was that she also planned to consume an inordinate amount of marijuana while in the tattoo chair. I didn't mind too much, because I was used to being around Lacey's weed by that point, but it was a bit awkward because I was the only person in the room *not* smoking. Even her tattoo artist was smoking.

"I'm Rev—short for Reverend," he said, extending an ink-covered hand to greet me.

"Why do they call you that?" I asked.

"Because I used to be one. I quit the ministry to be a tattoo artist."

Then he pulled up his T-shirt and showed me several tattoos of a bloody Christ and various Bible verses scattered across his shoulders. He smoothed his shirt back down and took the joint from Lacey, inhaling deeply.

I remember feeling halfway cool and halfway concerned, sitting in the middle of all those strange images, breathing in the smoke. *What would my parents think?* The room seemed cluttered and dark, and I felt like I wanted to crawl away ... to just quietly disappear from there, but I didn't really know why.

The tattoo turned out brilliantly, seven hours, $700, and five joints later. While we drove home, she insisted on listening to the Grateful Dead and some band where the lead singer had just died of a heroine overdose. The cliché and the irony were lost on me, in light of my admiration for Lacey and her new tattoo.

* * *

Shortly after Lacey and I became friends, I started noticing that any guy I professed a crush on was destined to be the next guy Lacey dated. She had an impressive confidence in everything she did, and guys loved it. She would loudly proclaim that she could drink more than any guy at the table, and she was always right. She could also eat mounds of food and never gain an ounce. She had the greatest body, the hippest apartment, the coolest dog, the sweetest tattoo, and a best friend who teetered somewhere between adoring her and secretly boiling with jealousy toward her. Crazy Lacey was practically flawless.

Then one day, someone told me that Crazy Lacey was bulimic. Then someone else told me. Then I heard her throwing up in the bathroom. I didn't say anything, and I kept trying to write it off as coincidence, which is something I did a lot with her. In fact, I tried to write off the fact that she, a professed vegetarian who recoiled at the sight of meat, always had chicken in her fridge. The pieces just didn't fit together anymore.

I grew increasingly frustrated with her lies and her attempts to be someone who she wasn't. I think I hated it so much because it mirrored what was happening inside of me. I rode her coattails into the dark places. I expected freedom and nonstop fun—and it was for a while. Then I began to feel desperate, like I was looking for hope in a place that offered none. I slowly started realizing that I hadn't found the perfect place of balance—I had over-corrected, veering so far to the left that I could barely see the lines of the road anymore.

The camel's back broke the day Crazy Lacey told me she was bringing a bus full of five-year-olds from her class to her apartment to finger-paint her hallway. There were about a million things wrong with this statement. First, I knew she wasn't allowed to paint her apartment. Second, she didn't have a bus driver's license. Third, their parents were allowing this? She addressed all my questions with answers that didn't really suffice, and I tried—again—to let it slide.

On the day of the big finger-painting extravaganza, she called me and gave me vivid descriptions of what they had painted on the walls. "The kids were so cute! They loved it! And it's really cool too—they drew trees and grass and giant pink clouds all through the hallway, and this one kid drew a green dog! It's so freaking awesome!" she said. Then she invited me over to help her fold some laundry and check out their masterpiece.

I pulled into the gravel driveway at her apartment and opened the door to the living room. She yelled out to tell me that she was in the bathroom, so I decided to explore on my own. I walked into the hallway to look at the artwork, but there was nothing there. Nothing. I scanned the bedroom and the kitchen, trying to give her the benefit of the doubt. Nothing. Not a drop of fingerpaint anywhere on the walls.

After she got out of the bathroom, she never mentioned it, so I didn't either. I was freaked out. I helped her fold the clothes, then as quickly as possible, I bailed.

I strategically avoided running into her. I never called her or returned her calls, either. In retrospect, this was probably the wrong approach, because I'm sure I should've offered more grace or something, tried to walk through the weirdness with her. Part of my bad response was likely a direct result of the fact that I hadn't been to church in nearly a year, and I didn't necessarily feel the tug of the Holy Spirit toward compassion. My callousness was coming in handy. I was selfish and angry and quite uneasy at the thought of her apparent alternate reality, so I wasn't too curious about "what Jesus would do."

* * *

It will find you when you beg and steal and borrow
It will follow you into a stranger's bed ...
So hold on—Love will find you
Hold on—He's right behind you now—just turn around.
—NICHOLE NORDEMAN, "Hold On"

For the next few months I still had no desire to go to church. I felt guilty, but not enough to do anything about it. After a while I started attending occasionally. Strangely enough, it wasn't the guilt of my new lifestyle that prompted this, but the feeling of my misplaced relationship with Jesus. I just ... *missed Him*, and I missed the way I felt when I was close to Him. God really knows how to cut to the chase. My new life, which I had strategically built to feed my own desires and comfort, left me *un*comfortable, actually. It was just a tiny feeling, but it was constant—like a pebble in my shoe.

I mustered up the motivation to attend a few of the college Sunday school classes, but they were unbelievably lame. The teacher could hardly get the class to stop talking, and when he did, the lessons were so simplistic that they might as well have been comprised of a flannelgraph and a juice break with animal crackers.

It had been so long since I'd been to church that I didn't want to waste my time in a class that wouldn't help me get back to where I wanted to be. Plus, I was fairly pretentious. So I joined the old ladies' class. I was the youngest person in the room by at least twenty years. The teacher was a lady named Judy, a tiny little woman with a personality bigger than Montana. Most of the women were divorced, tired, hurt, and scarred. I loved them.

They embraced me and prayed for me and begged me to learn from their mistakes. Suddenly, I had a room full of mentors who were eager to share their wisdom with me. (I like to think I helped keep them young, too.) One night we had a slumber party, and they bragged about how they planned to stay up all night like me. But after two hours, they decided they weren't built for all-nighters, so they pulled out their sleeping bags, unrolled them on the floor, and went to sleep. Thirty minutes later, they started getting up off the floor, one by one, and moving their sleeping bags onto beds because their backs were hurting. I saluted them for trying though.

After I spent more time with these ladies, a funny thing happened: I started discovering that I wanted to love God back. I felt so embraced by His family, so loved and wanted, not at all condemned for my late Saturday nights, my church-skipping ways, my pot-smoking friends, or my gradual theft of an entire entertainment center. And that made me want to love Him again—to actively start trying to talk to Him and understand Him again, because for the first time in a long time, I could feel and see His love for me, instead of just hearing about it.

4

Strange Beginnings

SHORTLY AFTER I STARTED GOING to church again, my Sunday school teacher Judy encouraged me to explore my musical interests, so I joined the college choir. They were desperate for altos, which meant that I didn't even have to go through the standard audition; I just had to promise to show up every weekday at noon, stay for an hour, and sing things in Latin. Considering my distaste for singing in languages I don't speak, I'm not sure why I agreed to join. It might've had something to do with the excessive number of hot guys in choir. It was ridiculous. The private liberal arts college was pretty big on athletics, so even the choirboys were jocks.

I was a second alto, so my seat was right next to the bass section. The first bass who was seated directly to my right was a beautiful, football-playing premed named Antonio. It was as if God smiled on me and dropped down this textbook-perfect man three feet away from me—a hunky brainiac with chin-length, curly, brown locks.

He loved Jesus, and despite that fact, he had somehow won the respect of everyone on campus, especially the people who weren't Christians. People talked about him with the same respect they'd afford Bob Marley, which to college students is huge. About halfway through our first conversation I realized that I wanted to be in choir for the rest of my college career, no matter what ancient songs they made us sing in foreign languages.

Antonio and I were quick friends. There weren't many Christians on campus, and I knew from the past year's experiences of stolen entertainment centers and nights hanging out with Crazy Lacey that I needed to spend more time with other Christians to help me not do stupid things like kiss boys I didn't even like. So Antonio and I hung out a lot.

Because his parents were missionaries in Russia, he didn't have much money or a car. So I carted him around a lot and loved every minute of it. The first winter he spent in Tennessee was a cold and snowy one, but he couldn't afford a coat. He had this belief that God would provide what he needed. One day, he got a North Face catalog in the mail, along with a $300 gift certificate with an anonymous note that said, "Buy yourself a coat." Incredible.

His relationship with Christ was one of those things that everyone knew about him immediately, not just because he lived it, but because he talked about it a lot. His philosophy was that Christianity is "show *and* tell." He didn't so much talk about how the rest of the world needed Jesus—he talked about how much *he* needed Jesus. It baffled the people who weren't Christians and left them with a head full of questions, because they were used to feeling like Jesus was being pushed at them instead of feeling pulled in by someone else's love for Him. In some strange sort of way, being around him made me love Jesus more too.

That was the first time I started to understand what the big deal was about being around other Christians and how it affects my love for Jesus. I had always been around tons of Christians, with or without trying, so I never had to be intentional about it. When I just let the chips fall where they may, bad things happened like they did when I hung out with Crazy Lacey. I think the enemy started putting people in my life who would make sin look pretty and enticing. And I believed the lie, at least for a little while. But being around Antonio reminded me of the truth: we are stronger when we are together.

* * *

I developed a monster crush on him, of course. People on campus started talking about whether or not we were dating. They started calling me his girlfriend. Girls who liked him started hating me (I loved it). People asked questions. And I didn't know how to answer them. While we were spending all of our time together, he hadn't made any declaration of his feelings or intent. This is a big problem in my life. I tend to fall for my friends, and then it gets all weird and confusing and I have no idea what to do.

In my experience, the inherent problem with male-female friendships is this: girls tend to fall for familiarity, and guys tend to fall for mystery. As the girl gets to know her guy friend better and learns about his character, he becomes more and more attractive to her; meanwhile, she becomes less mysterious and intriguing to him, and she slowly sinks into the quicksand of Just-Friends Land. I know that isn't always the case, but it seems to be fairly common.

According to my theory, I was doomed, because I knew by then that I was in love with him. I'd never been in love before, but I remember when it hit me—it was when he left for the summer to do missions work in Australia. I missed him so much that I swore my whole summer was being swallowed up into a black hole. I wanted to crawl into that hole and not come out until fall semester. It felt like I couldn't catch my breath for three months.

One day while he was gone, I was thinking about the size of the earth. I knew that the circumference of the earth is 25,000 miles, but the diameter is only 8,000 miles. Since he was practically on the exact opposite side of the earth, that meant he was roughly 12,500 miles away, if you measured around the earth. But if you measured straight through the earth to the other side, he was only 8,000 miles away, which was 4,500 miles closer. He was closer *through* the planet.

So I went to the valley behind my house and lay down in the deepest part of it, with my face to the earth, my heart beating into the dirt, and I felt somehow strangely comforted knowing that I was as close to him as I could possibly get at that moment. Love makes you do weird things.

> *The Mississippi's mighty, but it starts in Minnesota*
> *At a place where you could walk across with five steps down.*
> *And I guess that's how you started, like a pinprick to my heart*
> *But at this point, you rush right through me and I start to drown.*
> —INDIGO GIRLS, "Ghost"

* * *

When he returned for the fall semester, our friendship shifted into overdrive. We spent nearly every weekend together: we organized groups to go camping, ice skating, to concerts, to church. Most

Sundays after church, he ate lunch with my family, and my nieces and nephews adored him for all the time he spent with them.

Our relationship was suddenly too close for "just friends." The unspoken awkwardness prompted us to take turns pulling back from each other, but it was never long before we were inseparable again. One night we were fighting in my car, deciding whether or not to call off our entire friendship. Frustrated with the emotional roller coaster and unwilling to tell him that I was in love with him, I yelled at him to leave.

"Just leave—leave me alone!" I said. I didn't even look at him. Immediately, his voice dropped to nearly a whisper.

"Tara Leigh ..." he said tentatively.

"Go ... get out!" I said, pointing to the passenger door.

Then he turned to face me. The lights from the dorm parking lot spilled across the right side of his body. His face held no hostility, no anger—just tenderness.

"Can I hold you?" he asked.

"What?" I said, incredulous. I gripped the steering wheel.

"Look, I don't care who is right or who is wrong. I just know that you're hurting, and I want to hold you."

I crumbled. He broke me—not by strong-arming me or proving his point, but by gently showing me what love looked like: it is not self-seeking; it is not easily angered.

* * *

Loving him in silence was painfully difficult. If you are a girl and you want to be pursued, it stinks not to be able to say much about how your heart wants to explode every time you think about that person.

I stuck it out for a couple of years. I read *Passion and Purity* by Elisabeth Elliot about once a week to help me keep my mouth shut. The last thing I wanted to do was mess things up, and opening my mouth was a surefire way to do that. Falling in love with a good friend is a great thing and a true thing, because you know the real person and not the initial illusion, but the catch-22 is that the friendship feels too important to risk losing.

One night during his junior year, we went to see a play, then wound up talking for hours about the inappropriate closeness of our friendship. It was a terrible, frustrating talk that made me want to beat my head against the cinderblock walls of his dorm room. *Do we need to end our friendship? Pull back? What am I supposed to do now? I'm already in so deep.*

After much deliberating, he started saying strange new things to me. He told me that he loved me and wanted to marry me. *The room is spinning. My body is engulfed in flames.* He got on his knees and wept and thanked God for me out loud, right there in front of me. *Is this real? This can't be real. Please let this be real.* Then he stood up and held me, and we both cried. I didn't land for about eighty-seven hours.

It was real. And it was the single most breathtaking moment of my life. Everything I had waited for and hoped for and prayed for ... *finally.* Two years of silence and uncertainty were a small price to pay to spend my life with a man like him. I would've done it ten times over.

* * *

Then one November day, not too long after that, Antonio cornered me after choir and told me that we needed to talk. There was fear and pain in his voice, but he hid it well behind his resolve. He said that he knew it wasn't God's plan for us to be together because he believed he was supposed to be a single missionary. I was stoic as I stared past him at the brown leaves on the ground. *Everything is dying.* From the corner of my eye, I could see the wind blowing his hair. I couldn't meet his eyes because that would make it real, and then I might cry. And I could not cry, or I would dissolve. He walked away and left me standing in the freezing autumn air on the sidewalk outside his dorm, somehow still breathing.

It might sound to you like he was playing the "God Card," and I honestly wondered for a split second if he might've been, but I knew his character. I knew that he wouldn't have done what he did unless he really believed it was the right thing.

So, very reluctantly, I began to ask God to help me pry my fingers away from him. Mostly I asked God to change Antonio's mind, but sometimes I did ask Him to help me let go.

Antonio handled the whole situation with grace and kindness. I, on the other hand, was a little bit more of a jerk. In a vain attempt to try to plug the hole in the dam, I started dating this guy who was no good for me. I flaunted it in front of Antonio, just in case he had stopped missing me.

Antonio and I had never kissed because we had made this commitment not to kiss each other until the altar. That seems kind of stiff now, I know, but we were in college and trying very hard to be devout. So when I started dating this other guy, I brought him to the winter formal, and he kissed me on the dance floor when we were about five feet away from Antonio. I saw him look at us, then he dropped his elbows to his knees and covered his face with his hands. I felt some weird sense of gratification and searing pain all at once.

The next day, I broke things off with the other guy and resigned myself to the unavoidable pain of healing. I have never read my

Bible as much as I did during that time. I copied Scripture into my journal and read and reread it for comfort. It helped a little at a time. Nothing else did, really. God was honestly my only hope for recovery, and I knew that. I would say I clung to Him, except that I know that it was really Him clinging to me. I was too weak to cling.

It was a bad idea for me to be best friends with a guy—even a very, very good one who loves Jesus. Neither of us walked away unscathed.

* * *

The last time I saw Antonio was years ago, one sunny day in May at his graduation. Back when we were friends, he would bid me farewell by saying, "Have a nice life." And I always told him that I hated that because it sounded so *final* and that I would only say that to someone if I were done with him or her forever. He eventually stopped saying it to me, which I appreciated. We spoke briefly that day at commencement. My words were awkward and broken, fumbling in all the worst places. And as I was saying my disjointed, final goodbye to him, it almost slipped out. "Have a nice ... *stuff*," I told him, trying to recover. He winced, and I stammered, and then I walked past him and through the trees and cried in my car.

> *This is going to break me clean in two*
> *This is going to bring me close to you.*
> —THE FRAY, "She Is"

In the years since all of this happened, I still compare every man to him. Thankfully, some of them do measure up, because there are a lot of good men out there. Loving him changed me, but losing him changed me even more. I saw how much God wanted to hold my hand through all of it. He didn't always provide the answers to my questions, but He was always there. Psalm 34 says that God is close to the brokenhearted, and it's true. I have never felt as close to Him as when I lost Antonio.

I think God used it—the love *and* the pain—to help bring me here. That relationship was one of the biggest pieces in the picture of who I am today. It was the catalyst that hurled me, hurting, toward the better life that God had carved out for me.

Before the cracks started to seal even a little bit, I picked up a guitar for the first time ... to write songs of loving him and losing him and begging God to Send Help.

5

Long Shots & Short Cuts

THIS IS AN EXCERPT FROM *Grassroots Music Magazine*, which came out about twelve hours after I wrote the journal entry that follows it.

> *This week, Tara Leigh Cobble releases her newest indie project,* Things You Can't Stop with Your Hands. *I saw her perform these songs live a few months back, and was highly impressed by her progressive folk-rock style and lyrical sensibility. She's another artist I run into from time to time, one who's always hitting the road alone in her Toyota Camry, driving miles across the country for the chance to tell her story to those who want to listen.*

> *Tara Leigh seems extremely motivated in her music and doesn't appear to be lacking an ounce of self-confidence*

or certainty about her career. But if I had to bet money,
I'd guess she has moments of daydreaming too, wonder-
ing if the grass is greener someplace else. Or maybe that's
something everybody deals with ... even people who work
in places with elevators, their own cozy cubicle, and an
endless supply of Scotch tape.

Kierstin Berry
Editor, *Grassroots Music Magazine*

And here is the journal entry that I wrote the night before:

On my flight back from New York, I started reading a book
called Girl Meets God, *by Lauren F. Winner, which might*
as well be called Why I'm Better Than You. *In other*
words, I'm jealous of her. And surprisingly, it's not be-
cause this book makes me feel spiritually inferior, neces-
sarily. Most "Christian" books have a way of doing that,
a way of making me feel as though I'm not quite on par
with the author. I usually come away thinking, "I should
try to be more like that," which is the conscious transla-
tion of the subconscious thought, "Maybe God and/or
people would love me more if I were like that."

What's with all this unintentional grappling for love?
Make it stop. I know we're all built like that deep down ...
some kind of thing that opens us up to our Creator ... but
I'm awkward with it.

My pastor said the most profound thing in passing yester-

day, and I have tried to repeat it to myself a dozen times so far. He said, "God cannot love you any more than He does right now." In other words, no matter what stunts I master or how well I perform the balancing act, there is no more love to be had. And there's no less love for me when I fail. This is it. I am wrapped in Christ and loved infinitely. It's more, much more, than I understand. If I could just get that through my cerebrum, I'd be a lot better off. But I digress. Back to the book ...

The reason this book makes me feel somewhat inferior is mostly rooted in the course of my life. I'm not trying to venture off on a path of self-pity here at all, but I feel the need to be honest about it. The author's stories are the ones I wanted to live. It makes me wonder where I would be if I had not taken this route. Better yet, who would I be?

Would I have the life that I occasionally envy now? Would I be that girl—the one who wore the gorgeous cuffed black slacks, the long wool coat, and the Prada pumps at the post office today? Would I have gone to Harvard? Would I have lived in the City that I love so much that my heart breaks when I leave it? Why does Lauren F. Winner get to live the life I wanted? And the better question: why am I the ingrate who doesn't realize that a million people out there would trade everything for the chance to travel and sing their songs? For me, this is the paradox: the grass is always greener in the concrete jungle.

The timing of Kierstin's article could not have been more perfect. It showed up just in time to remind me that we all feel this way sometimes, no matter what job we hold or how ideal it seems from the outside.

* * *

Every night I meet at least one person who tells me that he believes God's plan for him is to be a musician. Based on the numbers of these kinds of encounters with the people at my shows, it seems like God must want *everybody* to be a professional musician. Does God ever call anyone to be garbage men or lawyers or secretaries? The situation also leaves me wondering if I should attempt to convey to these people what a musician's lifestyle is really like. Do they know what to expect if they *do* end up becoming a musician? I've learned from experience that any stories I tell of sleeping in my car and eating poorly and living month to month will only seem glamorous to the untrained ear and serve to reinforce their illusions.

In retrospect, I'm not sure I would've chosen this life had I known what I was getting into. It is exciting and fulfilling, but it is also harder than I ever imagined in every facet. I love my job—the nuts and bolts of it—but I hate the consequences of it.

Relationships and friendships are pretty close to impossible. Every single one of them is a long-distance relationship that requires great effort. I've found that most people aren't willing to make the effort, so I end up being alone even when I'm at home. Trying to eat well and sleep well and exercise is more difficult than solving the mystery of cold fusion. It's hard to remember what state I'm in, unless I look at the license plates on the cars that pass me. Bills pile up and late fees accrue and checks bounce and promoters cancel at the last minute with excuses like "We just don't have it in our budget right now."

Life on the road is excruciatingly lonely and alienating, and sometimes it feels like living in the movie *Groundhog Day*.

Every day I meet new people—wonderful, cool, boring, awkward, funny people. Despite how different they are, you can't help but notice that after a while, every conversation starts to sound exactly the same.

"Hi, what's your name? ... Nice to meet you, Brian. Where are you from? ... Colorado Springs? Fascinating ... And what's a boy from Colorado doing here at A&M? ... Wow, Brian ... really? What, exactly, do you plan to do with a major in political science and a minor in agriculture?"

Ad infinitum.

I spend thirty seconds getting to know three basic facts about each person. My relationship landscape starts to feel an inch deep and a mile wide. It's no fault of Brian, but I don't really know what to do about it. And suddenly, I'm splitting my time between Brian and fifty of his closest friends, learning bits about all of them.

Five years from now, I will meet Brian's roommate's girlfriend after a show, and she will come up to me and ask expectantly, "Do you remember me?" And she will think I am a jerk, because I probably won't.

But amidst the Groundhog Days, there has been one piece of grace that shows up from time to time and rescues me: over the years, I've met a few people who come to shows repeatedly—faces that I recognize, stories that I know, phone numbers that I've asked for and dialed. When those people show up, it is like someone is poking an air hole in the box where I live, pumping in oxygen. I feel myself lighten. I feel the corners of my mouth lift in a real way, not a forced way. Familiarity. Makeshift community.

It revives my soul. Without it, I probably would've left the road years ago.

Of course, being at home has its own problems. When I'm gone for weeks at a time, it becomes easier for my friends back home to forget that I exist. Parties happen. Relationships bloom. Movies are seen. Babies are made. And I come home to a whole new world every time, feeling more like a stranger than a native.

> *Living out this dream*
> *And wandering through fields of touch-and-go ...*
> *Tonight I want a life where the faces are*
> *the samemost every day ...*
> *I just want to land where the trees stand still.*
> —BEBO NORMAN, "Where the Trees Stand Still"

Last week I came home from being on the road for six weeks, and I had three days at home before leaving again for another four weeks. I made phone calls to let my friends know that I was coming back into town briefly, hoping that we could make plans to see each other. I missed them, needed them, wanted to know how their lives had changed in the past month and a half. I was caving in from being so lonely. But everyone either had plans or was on a tour of their own. My first night back in town was a Friday, and I sat at home by myself, reading until I fell asleep, fully dressed, on top of my duvet.

In my weaker moments, I can really feel sorry for myself. It's strangely encouraging when I meet other musicians who feel this sense of alienation. Even my friends who play on bigger tours tell me stories of being home for a week without their phone ringing. *At least I'm not the only one*, I tell myself. It's easy to get wrapped up in self-pity over the way that relationships on the road *and* at home don't seem to fill the void. But then there's the guilt you feel for feeling so ungrateful.

How ironic.

* * *

I never knew that I would end up being a musician. I had always kind of dreamed of it as a child while singing hymns in church. Song ideas started popping into my head somewhere around age five; the first full-length song I ever wrote was called "Happy Valentine's Day," and it was written to be a duet with my best friend at the time. I have books and tapes of the songs I've written over the years, stored in Rubbermaid containers in my basement. Most of them were terrible, but I didn't know it at the time. When Antonio broke my heart and I picked up the guitar, my songs started getting exponentially better. The cliché "broken hearts make for better art" was true in my case.

Then one day, about a month before my graduation, a youth pastor friend of mine asked me to play a few of my songs in a concert for his youth group. It was April Fool's Day. How fitting. I played for forty-five minutes to a group of kids who were kind enough to clap. That was when I felt like God was saying, "This is what you're supposed to do." And I was thinking, *Um, God ... were You watching the right show? Because that was not exactly what I'd call "good."*

The only way I can explain the weight of that calling is to say that it felt like God would not stop bothering me about it. It was that pebble in my shoe again ... the same feeling you might get if the cashier had given you way too much change at the store, and conviction weighed down on you until you had to return the extra cash. I felt like I didn't really have a choice. Nervous and excited and completely uneducated about what I was getting myself into, I obeyed.

Prior to that, The Plan was that I would graduate college, move to Dallas, and work as a flight attendant so that I could spend a few years seeing the world. Then I would eventually move back home to Greeneville to run my family's bookstore. I remember leaning over the bar in my kitchen on the day after my first concert and calling the airline to cancel the plans. As soon as I hung up the phone, I started making other calls—to everyone I knew who might have the power to get me a booking that summer.

I should mention that I had never even changed my own guitar strings. I didn't know how to tune my guitar, and—even more appalling—I didn't know when it *needed* to be tuned. Not to mention that the thought of sound checking made me want to crawl under something large and heavy. The only show I had ever played was the one on April Fool's Day. I was essentially an idiot.

But strangely, by the time I graduated college a month later, most of my summer had filled up with tour dates—churches, coffee shops, house concerts, camps, festivals. Then, by the end of summer, most of the fall had filled up with colleges and other venues. The rate at which God was opening doors was alarming. It felt like He really meant what He said—like He wasn't just messing around with me about this whole music thing. I alternated between feeling encouraged and terrified.

The biggest obstacle at this point, other than getting places to call me back and allow me to come play, was overcoming my dad's concrete opinions on my music. Mom was always encouraging, even when she was tentative, but Dad drew the hard line. I knew he didn't approve of "contemporary music" because he believed that drums were "the devil's music." And there I was, hoping to record an album with growling guitars and maybe even some drums (okay, a lot of drums). I nervously pressed on, begging God to Do Something.

Then God did this amazing thing that He does so well: He changed my dad's heart. It happened gradually, as he came to more and more of my shows—he started to smile occasionally while I played, started to tell me he was proud of me. I met a few of his friends who told me he had bragged on me behind my back. This is a man who doesn't clap at concerts because he doesn't want to give praise to the musicians. But somehow, God started shifting things inside of him.

Maybe He showed my dad that I wasn't trying to be famous, or maybe He simply let my dad see that there were lots of opportunities to share God's love with the people I met at shows—I don't really know what happened. All I know is that God opened the heaviest door with such beauty and grace and ease that I didn't have to do any pushing on my own. It made me love and respect my dad even more than I already did, and it made me understand God's purpose for me a little better, too.

That fall I boarded a plane with a ticket my parents had bought me and flew to Vancouver to record my first album.

There is a verse in Proverbs 21 that says that God is in charge of a man's heart and that He directs it like the water in a channel. I know this is true because of what God did with my dad. I want to honor him, and there's no way I could've moved forward in this without his approval. Ultimately, it was his emotional and spiritual support that helped carry me through the days when I ached to quit.

Again with the irony.

6

Touring Nineveh

EARLY IN MY CAREER, there was an abundance of what
I called "quitting days." In fact, every day for the first two years,
I begged God to release me and give me something else to do. I
hated it. I wrote a whole notebook full of songs about how much I
hated it. It felt like I was being swallowed up into the belly of the
whale and spit out on stage every night. I was miserable because it
wasn't glamorous, crowds were thin, and drives were long. But in
my weakest moments, when I was cursing my calling, God would
always provide something to sustain me.

One of my first big trips involved a three-day run through Mississippi and Louisiana. The show in Louisiana was the "anchor"
date, meaning that it was the one that actually paid for the trip. The
two shows in Mississippi were just "filler" dates that paid mini-
mally. I only booked them because I was already going to be in the
area. At the last minute, the anchor date pulled out. I didn't have a

deposit from them, and I knew I couldn't pay for the trip based on the filler shows. Thoughts of canceling the entire trip ran through my mind. I offered up frustrated prayers, and it felt like God was telling me to go play the filler shows anyway. Reluctantly, I went.

After I played the first show, the promoter pulled me aside and said, "We need to talk about the money." I cringed. This is the part where the promoter takes you into his office and throws some religious mumbo jumbo at you to help smooth over the fact that he isn't going to pay you.

"Well," he'd say, "things have changed. We've hit some hard times—there was a hole in the roof that we had to fix, and then our youth group's van broke down and we had to pay for the repairs so they can go on their trip to Disney World next month, so ... we're not going to be able to pay you this time. I hope you understand, sister. It's just that our budget is strained, and those are our priorities. I know that God will provide for you if you just trust in Him to do it."

I'd had conversations like that from time to time, and it always made me want to say, "Well, why don't you honor your commitment to pay me, and then *you* can do the 'trusting in God for provision' thing? I think He'll honor *you* more if you honor your commitment to pay me." I could never muster the guts to say it, though.

But that's not what this promoter said. He said, "You know what we agreed on financially? Well ..."

I could feel it coming. I shifted in my seat uncomfortably.

"We've been praying about it, and we feel like we should double it."

"Excuse me?" I sat up straight and furrowed my eyebrows, confused.

He smiled and said, "We just feel like God wants us to give you more than we promised you. Twice as much, actually."

After they resuscitated me, I started to see what God was doing. He was trying to get me to see that He would provide for me. He wanted me to learn to honor my commitments to play shows in the same way that I wanted those churches to honor their commitments to pay me. Even when the anchor shows pulled out, I still needed to go to the other places where He had opened the doors for me to play. It was a lesson that blessed me, as well as pointed the finger of conviction right back at me.

I was even more surprised the next night when the promoter at the other filler show pulled me aside and said they felt like God wanted them to double my honorarium too. I shouldn't have been surprised, but I was. And I could not believe the gratitude that God put into my faithless heart.

And all will be well
Even after all the promises you've broken to yourself
All will be well
You can ask me how, but only time will tell.
—GABE DIXON BAND, "All Will Be Well"

Between those two shows, they paid exactly the amount I would've made if all three shows had occurred. God made up the difference in His own way. People from those churches also told me they wanted to be regular supporters and send me money on a monthly basis. *Are you kidding me?* I don't understand a God who is humble enough to build my trust in Him. He doesn't have to earn it, because *He's God* and I should trust Him anyway ... but He was just loving enough to meet me there with my little bits of faith and help build it up piece by piece.

You can't learn these lessons in advance. You can only learn them in reverse, once you've walked through them. I guess that's why they call it "faith" on the front end.

* * *

God did other beautiful things too. He put these people in my life who stood beside me in my weakness and put their hands under my arms to hold me up. It was like when Moses had to hold his arms out over the Israelites when they were battling the Amalekites—as long as he did that, the Israelites would win, but anytime he let his arms down, they would start losing. So his friends came over and held up his arms for him when he was too tired and weak to do it himself.

Kemper Crabb is a man I had admired from a distance. He is a white-haired musical genius who played with one of my favorite bands, Caedmon's Call. He was also the A&R (artists and repertoire) director at Grassroots Music, which was the independent label/distributor that I considered to be "the brass ring."

My friend Todd plays in Caedmon's Call, too. One day I ran into him in Atlanta, and he introduced me to Kemper in a round-about kind of way. Desperate to impress him, I jabbered on and on about my adoration of Grassroots. Kemper probably thought I was crazy, but he was gracious enough not to call over The Guys in the White Suits.

A month later, Kemper left a message on my voice mail, telling me that they were interested in working with me. I called him back immediately. I think I dropped the phone twice during the conversation. And the voice mail stayed on my machine for more than two years.

He became my biggest defender, my biggest aide in the journey.

I had questions; he had answers. I wanted to quit; he had an army of reasons why I shouldn't. He'd present those reasons with a spoonful of sarcasm, which I loved.

"I hate this," I'd say. "I'm lonely."

"Paul was shipwrecked and beaten. Get over it."

"I'm not good at this," I'd offer. "I only know twenty chords."

"Moses stuttered, and God called him to lead a nation. He's bigger than your inadequacies. Besides, most hit songs only have three chords in them. You have seventeen chords to spare. Now, go write."

He was a guide and mentor to me in the most necessary times. It was like I was feeling my way through a dark tunnel, and he was there at the end, shining a light and saying, "*This* way. Crawl *this* way." There were days—many days—when all I could feel was an ache ... from not being good enough, from days' worth of unreturned booking calls, from writer's block ... and Kemper would answer my frantic calls with gentle pieces of hope. He poured out all his years of experience in the music industry to give me momentum for a journey that he knew would be long and tiresome. I knew that God had put Kemper in my life as a gift of grace.

* * *

Kemper also started strongly recommending certain books that he thought I should read. First on his list was the Lord of the Rings trilogy by J.R.R. Tolkien. I winced at the thought of it. I'm not much into fantasy stuff, but I picked it up anyway because he said so. I immediately began to associate Kemper with Gandalf, the book's heroic wizard with an honorable heart and all the right answers. That fit Kemper perfectly, so I started referring to him as "Gandalf." Later, I found out that other people had given him the same nickname, which only served to illustrate how fitting it was. Plus, he had the white hair.

In the first book, there is a part where Gandalf falls into an abyss, and Tolkien tries to make you think that Gandalf has died. Around the time I read that part, Kemper was grilling me about how far along I was in the book.

"Have you finished it yet?" he pestered me.

"No. Back off," I retorted.

"It's been a month since you started reading it! How far along are you?" he asked.

"I'm at the part where they are pretending that Gandalf died," I said.

"How do you know he *didn't* die?"

"Because they weren't sad enough," I replied. "If he had *really* died, everybody would've been more devastated."

I knew this because it did not match up to the amount of devastation I imagined that I would've felt if I suddenly had to make this journey on my own, without the wisdom that God kept passing along to me through Kemper.

For a while after reading that part, I went through this phase where I was terrified of losing Kemper as my mentor. *What if he dies?* I wondered. *How am I going to make the right decisions without him here?* I asked him to start writing down all the things that he thought were important, so that I could have them later, just in case. He reassured me that he had been doing that for years and that he had stacks of notebooks at home, full of his thoughts— surely those would get me by.

I can't imagine my life without a mentor. I am afraid of who I might have become, what decisions I would not have felt strong enough to make without his stubborn encouragement. God is a gracious, loving God for putting stronger Christians around me to hold me up—and I am sorry I didn't open my eyes to look for them sooner.

* * *

Over time, Kemper became kind of like a dad to me. A dad who listened to rock bands like Tool and A Perfect Circle, and who wore all black, even in the sweltering Houston summers. A dad with a wallet chain.

For my second album, *Home Sweet Road*, I asked him to be a co-producer (they make the big decisions about what happens on each song) and to play a lot of different instruments on it, too. He and I gathered with six other musician friends to record the album live during a concert at the Porter Center in Brevard, North Carolina.

Almost my entire family came to the show, which was a rarity. Jason, my funniest sibling, runs our family's lawn and garden center. Once, when I asked him about coming to see me play, he looked at me with a sort of fake shock and bewilderment in his eyes—the kind of look you'd give someone who offered to sell you his firstborn child—and said, "Why? I don't ask *you* to come and watch me sell lawnmowers, do I? Why would I want to come watch *you* work?" But even Jason came to my show at the Porter Center.

My dad came, too, even though there were drums and electric guitars. I knew he didn't like it, but I was so proud of him for being willing to tolerate it. It made me feel like he believed in my heart, even if he didn't like the particular style of music that came from the stage. I could not stop beaming.

During a break between songs, Kemper stepped up to the microphone assuredly, with his mandolin still strapped around his neck. He grabbed my mic as if it were planned and subdued a mischievous laugh as he said, "We'd like to dedicate all of the drum parts on this next song to Mr. Cobble." A strange combination of surprise and fear crept up inside me. I laughed nervously, and I heard my sisters gasp from all the way in the back of the auditorium.

After the show, my dad moved quickly to find Kemper. The two of them had never met, so I knew this first encounter wasn't going to be pretty. I saw my dad's brows furrow and his eyes narrow with intensity as he grabbed Kemper by the collar of his shirt, and in his most country drawl said, "Come here, boy." My dad made sure the *boy* came out solidly, with an air of condescension, even though he barely has a decade on Kemper. He pulled Kemper closer, using the fistful of black T-shirt he was gripping. I watched in horror. And then my dad's face softened, along with his voice, and he said, "I just want to thank you for all that you've done for my daughter. It means a lot to me."

My eyes covered over with water as I watched my worlds colliding: my fundamentalist upbringing of harsh opposition to modern music, and my mentor, who was the picture of that very thing. My guilt and fears from childhood stood face to face with the freedom of living out my calling, and they were—beautifully, unexpectedly—at peace with each other. I was overcome with relief and swept up by encouragement that sustains me still. In my mind, I have highlighted that memory in indelible ink.

In the midst of my desire to run fast and far from my calling, God gave me this beautiful gift. He's like that, you know. I think they call it "grace."

"Paradigm"
(For Gandalf)
—TARA LEIGH COBBLE

Verse 1:

You are pulling at the edges of all of my horizons.
Now the sun sets all around me every day.
Now the moon spins all around me every day.
You say you want me to be whole and wise.
And He has sent a cloud to lead the way.
And He has sent a fire to lead the way.

Chorus:

And you are crowned with wisdom
Multiplied through time ...
And everyone leans in ...
Closer to the paradigm ...
Closer to the paradigm.

Verse 2:

Someday I will make it to the mountain,
But sometimes I can't find the forest for the trees.
And I can't make it through the forest for the trees.
So I call for answers and you call for grace.
And your answers are Wind in the Wheat.
He answers with Wind in the Wheat.

Bridge:

And we wonder aloud how you got to this place ...
Have you ever seen less than His face?

7

JANE AND I HUNG OUT two or three times after we met at one of my shows in east Tennessee. Shortly after that, I left on a four-month spring tour to promote my second album, *Home Sweet Road*. Somehow, she got in touch with just about everyone I'd ever met in my life and had them secretly write me notes of encouragement. She collected them all and presented them to me on the day before I left for the tour: two bags overflowing with nearly two hundred cards and letters.

No one had ever done anything like that for me before. I was incredulous. I think it was her deliberate effort of generosity—combined with the fact that she seemed normal and not at all stalker-y—that made me want to be friends with her.

One night after a show, we wound up playing a game of Cranium. Jane was on a team with my road manager, Susan, and I was on a team with my percussion player, Alan. We played for nearly four hours, and we finally decided to call it a night just as the sun was creeping up. In the final round, Jane had to act out a character, and Susan was supposed to figure out who it was, based only on charades.

Jane put a finger above her lip, as if to simulate a mustache, and began to raise and lower her eyebrows quickly, while walking around the room in a wobbly fashion. It was *clearly* Charlie Chaplin, although other acceptable answers (based on my description) would've been Hitler or Groucho Marx. Alan and I both knew it immediately and whispered it to each other behind cupped hands so Susan couldn't hear us. For some reason, she wasn't picking up on it at all. She began to shout out ideas:

"Connie Chung! ... Jackie Chan! ... Um ... Bruce Lee! Uh ... Connie Chung! *Connie Chung!*"

Jane dropped her fake-mustache finger and started laughing, gasping for breath. "Pretend I'm not Asian!" she said. "I'm not *acting* Asian so that you'll guess the character! I just *am* Asian!"

That is when I began referring to her as "Pretend I'm Not Asian Jane." It was one of the most hilarious things I've ever witnessed. My abs ached from laughing, and I hoped that Jane and I would be friends for a long time.

* * *

A few years into our friendship, there was a night when Jane and I were sitting in my car outside a Starbucks where we had lingered past closing time. We wound up in a conversation about how frustrating it is to not understand what God is doing in our lives. I was trying to decide when to move to Nashville, and Jane was bemoaning a job that didn't make her feel alive inside.

"I know it's where God has me right now," she said. "But I hate it. I want to be *through* this phase of life. I want to just speed right through it and come out on the other side."

I knew what she meant. I couldn't wait to get my feet on city soil; it seemed like the move to Nashville couldn't come quickly enough. Even though I knew it was looming ahead, waiting for it was like waiting for your meal to arrive at a restaurant where everyone else is eating and you're starving. The anticipation frustrates every breath.

"I'm sure there's a reason for this timing," I tried to console her. "In ten years, you'll probably look back and understand *exactly* why God had you in this job at this time. This is an integral part of your journey to some better place. We don't understand it now, but I'm sure it'll make sense later."

I was worried that I had doled out too much of the "We may not know what tomorrow holds, but we know Who holds tomorrow" rhetoric. While it's true, it's a hard truth to hang on to when you want everything to be mapped out and to make sense. As I said it, I also thought about how much I wanted Jane to be happy, because she is one of those people who rains down generosity and selflessness into the lives of others. I couldn't understand why God wasn't calling her to move on yet, why He was leaving her in this frustrating place. We didn't have a choice but to wait for Him to Do Something and move her into the next phase of her life.

That's when Jane said it—the phrase that has become part of my daily vocabulary, that has helped remind me that God is trustworthy even when I don't get Him *at all*—and she said it better than I ever could have, despite the fact that I am the songwriter and she is in the business world.

"Well, then ... *here's to hindsight*."

I nodded in dumbstruck agreement, and we lifted our nearly

empty cups of cold coffee and toasted to the present—our past yet-to-come.

It's a toast we both still use, because it feels like a toast to God. "I don't understand You," it says, "but I know You're doing something good here."

8

Highway Miles
-Exit 1

Nationwide: June—July 2001

PERHAPS I SHOULD'VE THOUGHT it through more: a six-week national tour, with three people, three guitars, a djembe, merchandise, clothes, and camping equipment—*in a Camry*. On the day that Susan, Brad, and I were packing up to leave, my parents told me that I must've been smoking crack to think that we'd fit everything into my little car. Those weren't the exact words they used, but you get the gist. They graciously offered to let us use their minivan. And let me tell you—that's a surefire way to look cool when you pull up to the venue: *parents' minivan*. Right. Nonetheless, I was grateful.

Brad insisted on driving most of the time. Due to the fact that he never rode in the passenger's seat, he didn't see the need to clean that side of the windshield. In fact, he refused to let me or

Susan clean it either. As soon as he threw the van into "park" at a gas station, he would leap from the vehicle and steal all the squee-gees at the gas pumps. After about a week of driving cross-country, the half of the window in front of the steering wheel was immacu-late. The other half—my half—looked like it had been painted. He seemed to think that was a fun game to play: *Keep Tara Leigh from Seeing America.*

I was glad to have him along, though. I asked him to join the tour to play djembe, and also because I thought he'd be a safe male option, meaning that I was pretty sure I would never be attracted to him, and therefore never inadvertently throw the tour into Fleet-wood Mac-like territory. And I was right. I was totally unattracted to him for the entire first two days of the tour.

It was all downhill from there. We started to fight a lot more. That could just be normal road tension, but probably not. It was probably more related to the fact that I wanted him to kiss me. He drove and listened to Ben Harper and O.A.R. and Weezer, while I pretended to sleep in the passenger's seat but secretly watched him from behind my sunglasses, wondering what it would be like to put my fingers in his hair.

* * *

Northeast, Midwest: January—April 2002

The "Three-Week Wall" is what I call the time when your body refuses to be on tour anymore and tries to escape at any cost. It's when all systems shut down, you get sick, and you wish to be anywhere but where you are. This is usually the time when band politics start to grate on everyone's nerves. It's when "people stop being polite and start getting real," as they say on *The Real World.*

Susan was road-managing for me on a four-month tour through twelve states, and I remember when we hit our wall. Physically, I hit mine early and quickly. I got sick with some kind of cold/flu thing before a show in Ohio, but it only lasted for a day. Zicam is my favorite cold remedy in the world because it kicks germs in their faces and leaves them moaning on the ground like little babies.

Susan managed to pass her wall pretty quickly too, and it's always great when everyone can get past the wall simultaneously, so that the stragglers don't pull down the people who have already healed. Germs love to re-circulate like that. Jerks.

"Wall time" is always stressful for me, because I'm just waiting, wondering, hoping it will end soon without much consequence and without resurfacing. After the wall, Susan and I were getting along fairly well, which is huge. I'm fully aware of the fact that I am much more difficult to live with than most people, being so passionate and opinionated. She was the fulcrum, and that's never easy on a person. I learned a lot just from being around her constantly and being the recipient of so much grace. When you live with someone twenty-four hours a day, eating every meal together, driving together, and sometimes even sleeping in the same bed, you get pushed beyond your comfort zone pretty quickly.

Touring can be a bit like mountain climbing in that there are a lot of uphill struggles, a lot of steep cliffs ... and it's usually not until the whole thing is over, when you've reached the peak, that you can look back on it and breathe in the beauty of it all. It's too much of a struggle during the ascent, too steep of a climb to stop to look around and realize what an amazing gift it all is.

Some of the things in touring life that have been the biggest deals to me have, in reality, not really amounted to much. For some reason, living in that environment with other people causes lack of perspective. For instance, halfway through the tour, Brad decided to leave. I was pretty sure our friendship would never recover. But six months later, we were hanging out again. Last weekend, I went to his wedding. It's easy to make too big a deal out of things that really aren't earth-shattering. I'm starting to wonder if it's because of the lack of stability, the lack of routine. The slightest thing can throw you off, especially if you're Type A, like me. I am a big fan of knowing exactly what is going on, so any unexpected change is usually met with resistance.

When Susan and I had been on the road for nearly four months straight, one of those changes happened. We were in the last stretch of shows. Four days before I was supposed to play the last show, they canceled. That meant we were going to be home three days early. You'd think this would've made me ecstatic, but it didn't. My first response was to be frustrated and worried about when I could make up for the financial loss. But when I stepped back and summed up the situation, I started to get really excited about going home early.

At that point, my focus shifted, appropriately, toward home—I couldn't wait to be there. I suddenly realized how much this all parallels my spiritual life. Sometimes I get so wrapped up in the weight of life that I lose my perspective, I get frustrated, and I forget that I'm on my way Home. Even when things get messed up, even when there are struggles, I'm on my way Home. Somehow I forget that I'm looking forward to it.

* * *

Topeka, Kansas: February 2002

The Weather Channel said it was seventeen degrees in Topeka. I was thoroughly anticipating that, as Susan and I had spent the last month being followed around the country by snowstorms. I'm a pansy when it comes to cold weather; I don't like any temperatures that start with a number less than seven. In fact, I protested the cold by bringing only one sweater for our three-week stint in the Northeast that February, hoping that would somehow convince God that He should alter the weather for my benefit. But He did not concede.

We drove from Cleveland to Topeka in one day. By the time we hit Topeka, so had the snow. Of course.

I spent the off-day milling around town alone. I drove the streets listening to "Superman" by Five for Fighting on repeat. It comforted me as I navigated that unfamiliar town with the heat cranked up inside the car. I pulled over when I saw Giant Monopoly Bookstore (names have been changed to protect the money-hungry).

Truth is, I love those bookstores. They are the places that most closely resemble home. If I feel homesick or frustrated, just get me to a bookstore quickly, and I'll be fine. My parents have owned a bookstore all of my life, and that infused my love for books at a young age. In fact, my favorite week of the year was always in the middle of summer when we would go to the international booksellers convention. We'd come home with boxes full of new books and CDs for me to explore during the coming year.

Every time I step into a bookstore, I feel the comfort of being where I belong. There is also something incredibly humbling about being surrounded by all that information.

I stood in the religion section, scanning all the books for evidence of which one might be entertaining or hold some bit of truth that I needed to learn. The religion section is the most bipolar of all sections: so full of wisdom, so full of crap. The wooden walls of book spines overwhelmed me, but I finally managed to find a John Piper book that called my name.

Usually, if I spot something in the religion section that appeals to me, I'll buy it from a Christian bookstore instead. I'm biased, but it just seems like a good way to be a better steward of my money. But that night I broke my rule, since the local Christian bookstore was already closed and I was leaving town the next day. I picked up my book and headed back out to face the snow.

As I drove out of the parking lot, I stopped for a minute to watch the loose, fallen snow blow across the parking lot in swirls and streams ... it was mesmerizing. It made me wonder if God is in the process of redeeming winter for me. He keeps showing me simple, beautiful things about it. Like the way I still get excited about seeing my breath when it's cold. And the way I love to watch snowflakes fall in the city at night. We'll see. I'm not sold on it yet.

* * *

I been speaking later and later in the day.
Most days I don't talk 'til maybe eight o'clock at night.
—DAN BERN, "Black Tornado"

West Coast: June—August 2002

It took me eight weeks, but I trekked from east Tennessee to California and back again by myself. Most of the trip westward was a blur, until Arizona. My first complete memory is of leaving Tucson—it was either Tucson or the surface of the sun—but I left just moments before my flesh melted.

At the time, I had a CD player that would only play burned CDs. Whenever I bought new CDs, I couldn't listen to them until

I arranged to make a duplicate. It annoyed me beyond belief. My friend Tamara lives in Tucson, and she offered to burn me a copy of the Counting Crows CD I had just gotten. To this day, that CD reminds me of driving in the smothering heat from Tucson to San Diego. I like to listen to it when the dead of winter starts weighing down on me, and I can close my eyes and feel happy again, just remembering what Death Valley feels like in July.

That journey from Tucson to San Diego involves a long stretch of the hottest desert in North America, the Sonoran Desert. Everyone offered fierce warnings before I left: *Fill up on gas! Take a few gallons of water! And food, too ... don't forget food! And have you had your malaria shots? Wash behind your ears!*

I survived the desert and the sand dunes, and made my way to see my very first San Diego sunset. The night proved flawless. I caught the sun sinking into the ocean from Mission Bay. It devastated me, it was so beautiful. I walked out onto the sand, and there were people sitting all along the beach on the backs of trucks, standing in the sand, singing along to guitars and stereos, laughing with their friends in that beautiful, suspended moment.

I'd never seen anything like that in real life. It felt like a scene from every movie I had watched in high school. I wanted to join the people in their circles of friends, but opted instead to just take off my Chacos, roll up my jeans, and step into the Pacific on my own. Then I had a strange feeling that I'm not quite sure how to express—it was almost painful to try to handle that much beauty alone. It overwhelmed me, really. I drove back to my hotel room and fell asleep without saying a word to another human being that day, except for the lady behind the desk at the hotel.

* * *

> *I don't mind the days gone rolling away*
> *'Cause all this sunlight feels warm on my face today.*
> *But what brings me down now is love*
> *'Cause I can never get enough.*
> —COUNTING CROWS, "Goodnight, L.A."

California: July 2002

I found myself in Southern California without a show for three whole days. Not only did that mean I'd be alone for at least seventy-two hours, but it also meant I'd be paying for a hotel room for three nights. I had been alone for most of the past week, and my mouth was starting to seal over from lack of use. So I decided to drive up to San Francisco and visit my friend Sam, who also agreed to put me up for the night.

Sam used to play in a band called Dime Store Prophets, which I listened to in college. After they broke up, he started running sound for lots of other musicians. That is how I came to know him. He's very bookish and opinionated, but not in an overbearing fashion, which appeals to me. And if anyone can empathize with a heart that is road-weary, Sam can. So I drove up to San Francisco, excited about his promises to show me the city and take me out for an unbelievable meal.

He delivered on both. We ate at Nanking, a hole-in-the-wall Chinese restaurant that usually has a line around the block. As we were walking there, Sam told me that the owner always wears striped shirts. I couldn't wait to see if he was right. Sure enough— blue-and-orange horizontal, with a white collar.

The guy is like the Soup Nazi from *Seinfeld*. If you order something he doesn't want you to have, he won't give it to you. Sam knows all the tricks about eating there, so he ordered for both of us. And I don't know if it was luck or skill, but he happened to order exactly what I would've ordered for myself. We ate General Tso's chicken, steamed broccoli, and brown rice from faded yellow platters as we traded road stories and Sam told me about the books he was reading.

It was getting cold after dinner—because it is cold in San Francisco *all the time*—but we embarked on our tour of the city nonetheless. I'd been there a few times before but had never really had much time for sightseeing. I bought a pair of Tevas there a few years ago, and that's my main memory of the city—well, that and riding the cable car. Sam took me to see Lombard Street, which is the curviest road in America and goes downhill at a pretty steep angle. It's also where MTV's *Real World* house was when Puck was on the show.

My one request was that we visit the Palace of Fine Arts. I had always seen that place in movies and pictured it in my mind as some kind of glorified gazebo. I was so completely off—it is huge, and it is spectacular. I highly recommend it. Also, there are ducks.

Sam lived with four other people, and through some strange coincidence, a couple of those people had also invited other musicians to spend the night there in the midst of their respective tours. So there were fourteen of us, packed onto couches, air mattresses, floors, and beds. And there were lots and lots of tattoos. Everywhere.

The next morning when I woke up, I had no idea where I was headed. I just threw my stuff in the car and started driving in the prettiest direction. I ended up in downtown San Francisco, and I just kept going. That led me to Highway 1, which was just perfect. Highway 1 is a winding two-lane that goes down the West Coast, right beside the ocean. It's in a lot of car commercials and sev-

eral episodes of *90210*. In what I now refer to as the Year of the
Tevas, I drove Highway 1 from Humboldt (in Northern California)
down to San Francisco. That part of the highway is scattered with
Redwood trees and my favorite flowers, calla lilies. It was captivat-
ing, so I had been hoping for an opportunity to drive the southern
stretch. That three-day break was my chance.

I spent the next couple of days driving down the coast, sometimes at a lazy pace, sometimes hurrying to get to the next town. I
watched the sun set in the golden Pacific from the top of a grassy
hill south of Monterrey, where there wasn't another person in sight.
And I ate at little outdoor cafés that perched above rocky cliffs
along the ocean. I read books and wrote songs and watched *Late
Night with Conan O'Brien* three times each day and slept in. It was
like a honeymoon with myself, which meant that it was amazing
but also terribly lonely. In my king-sized bed each night, I thought
about how part of me wanted to be back in San Francisco, sleeping
on an air mattress, surrounded by tattooed musicians who snored
and smelled.

9

Travel-Sized

THE ROAD AND HOME are two different animals, but both of them beat me into submission. And whichever place I am has convinced me that that's where I want to stay. After I've been gone for a long time, it starts to feel like there's not much to come home to. And after I've been home for a few days, it's excruciating to have to pack my things back up and leave my wonderful Tempur-Pedic mattress again.

I spend my days at home booking shows, assembling press kits, washing the three outfits that I wore on tour that month, replying to emails, writing songs, recording demos of those songs, opening piles of overdue bills, throwing out food that has not outlived its expiration date, refilling the travel-sized bottles of everything I own for when I leave again, and trying to see my friends in the midst of all that. Home knows no schedule.

But just so you can have an idea of what a normal day might

look like on the road, I'll give you the rundown:

8:00 a.m.: Housekeeping begins knocking on the door, completely ignoring the "Privacy Please" sign that I left on the door handle. I tell them I'm staying until checkout.

9:00 a.m.: Housekeeping knocks on the door again. I don't reply. I hear them sticking the key card in the door, and I mentally defy them to open the door, knowing full well that I've locked every possible lock. There is no way they can get in, barring the use of explosives. I roll over and go back to sleep. Again.

10:00 a.m.: The alarm clock blares. I peel my eye mask off my head and remove my earplugs. When I stay at hotels, I often fall asleep while watching movies on my laptop. So I'll wake up with the menu playing over and over, "This is Part 7 of *New York: A Documentary Film* by Ric Burns, presented by PBS ..."

10:05 a.m.: I plug in my travel blender (which is actually just a regular blender, made of chrome so it weighs about the same amount as the engine block of my car) and make my protein shake. I get ready, check email, and pack up while watching some combination of CNN, *The View*, and Fox News. Now that Bill Hemmer is on Fox News, I don't have to get up at the crack of dawn to see him on CNN anymore. It was extremely courteous of him to switch networks out of consideration for my sleeping habits and my giant crush on him.

11:00 a.m.: I leave the hotel. Actually, this happens around 11:15, when housekeeping begins pounding on the door yet again, explaining that I'm fifteen minutes late for checkout and that they will have to charge me for an extra day if I don't leave *right now!* And they'll also put it on my "permanent record," and I'll have a hard time getting into a decent college someday if they find out that I can't even check out of my hotel room on time!

11:15 a.m.: Run any errands that I might have. This could include stocking up on food and bottled water at the grocery store, going to the post office to mail promotional materials to venues, getting my acrylic guitar nails done, going to the bank, getting an oil change, whatever. If my hotel did not have Wi-Fi, this is when I scramble to find a place to log on to the Internet and check my email.

12:15 p.m.: After attempting to decipher the map, I assuredly pull out of the parking lot, making certain to hit the curb first, then I wind up going the wrong way on a one-way street. Never fails.

12:19 p.m.: Usually at this point, I'm driving (the correct direction) while simultaneously beginning a fun-filled day of bookings. I have a few people who work in my office occasionally, and I make these phone calls at the same time they do. We make several calls back and forth while also calling the venues, just to make sure we're not double-booking any dates. Depending on how the call to the venue goes, we will get one of three responses:

1. "I've overestimated our budget and will not be able to book you."
2. "I've underestimated our schedule and will not be able to book you."

3. "I'm really interested in booking you, but I have to take this before 'The Board.' Call me back next week, at which time I will tell you that I forgot to take it before The Board, and I'll ask you to call back in another week, at which time I'll tell you that I took it to The Board and we all decided that, despite our encouraging talks with you over the past five months, your chances of getting a booking here are about the same as your chance of being selected to join NASA on the next mission to the moon. So don't ever call us again. Oh, and by the way, *God bless!*"

2:30 p.m.: Stop for lunch at Taco Bell. "Two crunchy tacos and an ice water, please." Eat while driving.

5:00 p.m.: Arrive at the venue. (If this day happens to be a day where I don't play a show, then I could be driving for up to eighteen hours.) Meet the promoter. Begin load-in. That's the part where I carry in my guitars, my giant load of merchandise, and anything else I might need for the show that night.

5:15 p.m.: If people are helping me carry things in, this is usually when I finish load-in. I begin stage and merchandise setup and train any merchandise volunteers who might be helping out at the show.

5:30 p.m.: Ideally, begin sound check. Depending on how much experience the soundman has with the particular soundboard he is operating, this can take anywhere from three minutes (my fastest ever) to two hours (my slowest ever). Typically, it takes fifteen to thirty minutes.

6:00 p.m.: Grab dinner—hopefully something healthy. This is usually my only opportunity to eat an actual meal. Depending on where we're eating, this could take anywhere from ten to ninety minutes.

7:30 p.m.: Get back to the venue for final preparations. Make sure the sound system is still working and that no merchandise has been stolen in my absence.

7:45 p.m.: Go into seclusion to gather my thoughts, pray, and write out the set list for the night. If I'm not able to go into hiding, I usually tie up any loose ends and maybe meet some people who are getting there early for the show.

8:00 p.m.: Typical showtime. Depending on opening acts, length of sets, intermission, etc., the show could last anywhere from an hour to three hours, but it's usually between ninety minutes and two hours.

10:00 p.m.: Show ends. I begin the meet-and-greet while working the merchandise table.

11:00 p.m.: Venue clears out. I start tearing down the merchandise table and the stage. People offer to help, but I refuse to let them because I have it down to a science and don't want to sound like the Packing Nazi. I ask them to just keep me company and help me carry things out to the car.

11:15 p.m.: Kind people help me carry things to the car, and then I either hang out with friends or go to my hotel room. Let's pretend that this is a night where I'm hanging out with friends.

11:30 p.m.: Go to wherever my friends are. It might be a restaurant, a Waffle House (not to be confused with a "restaurant"), or someone's house.

1:30 a.m.: Arrive at the host home or hotel room. If it's a host home, I will probably talk with the hosts for a while (if they're still awake), but if it's a hotel room, I immediately get ready for bed. At this point, I'm pretty beat. The adrenaline has worn off, and I'm just ready to recharge. I feel relaxed until I realize that I missed *Late Night with Conan O'Brien.*

2:00 a.m.: If I have Wi-Fi, I check email and reply to anything that seems urgent.

2:45 a.m.: Watch clips from *The Daily Show* online. I laugh a lot and wish that Jon Stewart could go on tour with me and do a running commentary on everything that happens because he is the single funniest individual alive, except for Conan O'Brien.

3:00 a.m.: Read a book, read my Bible, and pray that God will help me fall asleep sometime soon, please.

4:00 a.m.: My body finally gives in to the fact that I must sleep occasionally.

8:00 a.m.: I hear that familiar, "Housekeeping!" at my door again ...

10

Newfound Friends

NASHVILLE IS LIKE AN AMAZING GUY that I love, who just doesn't love me back anymore. "You're so great!" I tell it. "I love you! Let's spend some time together!" Then it stands me up and doesn't return my calls.

New York City, on the other hand, sends me flowers every day. It pursues me and woos me and wants to meet my folks. It calls me frequently when I'm on the road, comes to my shows when I'm in town, and begs me to move there.

This past month, I took a long walk through Hillsboro Village, my neighborhood in Nashville. I walked down the brick sidewalks, past the trendy shops and hip restaurants, under the tiny trees bedecked with twinkle lights. Then, with sadness in my voice, I told Nashville that I think I want to start seeing other cities.

I've started mentally preparing myself for a potential move to New York City. I've been physically preparing, too. Every day that

I am home in Nashville, I go through a drawer or a box and choose a few things to get rid of. I can't take everything with me if I move. Right now I live in a pretty big house with tons of storage, and I'm sure that any place I can afford in New York City will be roughly the size of a jail cell.

There are five grocery bags stuffed full of clothes sitting on my hardwood floor right now. Tomorrow, they're going to Goodwill. And tomorrow, I'll be five bags closer to my probable new city. I don't know for sure that I'll move, but I *think* I will. I'm going to give Nashville one last push—to see if I can really live here anymore, because I really do love it, but it just doesn't love me back. If this last desperate attempt doesn't work, I'll take it as a hint that I'm meant for other places.

* * *

Nashville hasn't always been a hard place for me to be. There was a time when it was the most glorious place on earth. I moved here three years ago because all my closest friends lived here; it was merely coincidental that Nashville is Music City (that has been an added bonus, but wasn't a factor in my decision-making process). Primarily, I came to Nashville because I needed to be around young single people, and Greeneville didn't provide that option. (When people from my hometown move away for college, they don't come back.)

I started to notice that life was moving and I was standing still there. I was sinking, actually. I could feel God pulling me out, slowly at first—then, all of a sudden, I looked around and I was free. And I knew that I was supposed to use that freedom to move somewhere away from Greeneville. It was that same feeling I had when I started playing music for a living—this quiet, persistent urging to step out, to follow something that I couldn't quite see but was helpless to ignore.

I prepared myself to be emotional, to cry during the entire four-hour drive from Greeneville to Nashville with my whole life in tow. But I never did. I got choked up once, as I turned onto my new street and the Dixie Chicks' version of "Landslide" came on the radio. "I've been afraid of changing / 'Cause I built my life around you / But time makes you bolder / Children get older / I'm getting older too," they sang. I knew that I was afraid of changing, and I knew that I was getting older.

Leaving behind everything I knew, moving to "the big city," watching my parents fade further away, I felt like I had nothing to stand on. Like all familiar foundations were being ripped out from under me. I wondered if I was making a mistake, but felt like I had to move in order to avoid getting pulled under again.

As the chorus finished, I pulled into my new driveway and saw that I already had friends waiting there to help me unload the fifteen-foot moving truck. There were nearly twenty of them— friends from my new church, acquaintances from shows, friends of friends—all sacrificing their time to help the new girl feel at home. Christine and Kelly and Meredith, who are three of the main reasons that I moved to Nashville, organized most of the process and made sure that I was settled by the end of the night.

Sometime around midnight, I climbed into my fully assembled bed, in a room where my clothes sat neatly folded in drawers and paintings hung on the white walls, thanks to my group of friends. As I pulled my duvet up to my chin, I thanked God for bringing me to a place where I had community. He somehow managed this trick where I lost nothing on the path to gaining a whole new world.

* * *

The transition wasn't too hard on me because I had spent a good amount of time visiting Nashville beforehand, building friendships and finding a church. At that point, I just had to sink my heels in. I stayed off the road for the first few months, only playing short tours, which allowed me to be home long enough to let the concrete of my new foundation dry.

It didn't take me long to find out that my new friends were pretty big fans of community, too. We went out to eat every Sunday after church; we grabbed food to go at Calypso Café and took it for a picnic in Centennial Park, then played volleyball and Frisbee. We usually planned one or two fun activities during the week, too—movies or game nights or going to each other's concerts. My friend Jeremy started an email listserv to make sure everyone got included in the up-to-the-minute plans. They made it easy for me to fall into place with them. The transition to my new world was seamless.

> *Turns out not where but who you're with*
> *That really matters*
> *And hurts not much when you're around.*
> —DAVE MATTHEWS BAND, "The Best of What's Around"

* * *

When one of my friends started dealing with some tough addictions, it stretched me for the first time in a long time. That's when I began to realize that maybe this whole notion of "community" wasn't just about *me* having friends ... maybe it was about *them* feeling loved too. Maybe that is the way that iron starts to sharpen iron—the initial contact. Maybe I wasn't just getting a community, but getting an opportunity to *serve* a community, to love people back, to love them just because they are humans like me, with their own broken hearts and insecurities and fears about the future.

I decided to join a Bible study to plug in and make my friendships a little more authentic—to let my friends see my ugly sides that I tend to hide from the general public, especially small children and refined ladies with sweater sets. It seemed natural to assume that any Bible study group in its right mind would need a gun-wielding (hey, I'm from the South), small-town musician to help round things out nicely. So when Stephanie invited me to join her group, the Tuesday Night Jesus Club, I immediately accepted and fired a few celebratory rounds into the air.

First, though, she warned me, "You really need to decide whether or not you're going to commit to it. If you're not going to, then don't even come." Her words were daunting, because I was still pretty new to Nashville and had never been to TNJC. The group was made up of girls from a few different churches, mostly single girls in their twenties. "We've had so many people come and go, and that makes it hard to dig in and invest in each other, so you should probably pray about it a lot before you make a decision," she added.

I understood, so I prayed about it. And on my first Tuesday night there, twenty of us gathered in Amber's cramped apartment and started working through a book called *Strong Women, Soft Hearts.*

Within an hour, I was hooked. Within a month, the group started to thin a bit, as Stephanie had warned. Eventually, the group narrowed down to six of us. Six was a great number, in my opinion—just big enough to make it interesting, but small enough that you could really open up to knowing people and being known. Plus, it left time for each of us to share our weekly dirt, which is always a favorite social activity among females. Tuesday quickly became my favorite night of the week.

Amber, whose husband Matt designed my last album cover, is one of the most stunning people I've ever met. I hated her when I first met her, because I did not believe that she could possibly be that nice *and* that hot. But she is. Shannon, who is married to Jeremy, rubs my shoulders when they hurt from driving too long on tour. They are one of the coolest couples I've ever met, and he even took the pictures for my last album cover. Jenny is brilliant and gentle, and it wouldn't surprise me if she were related to the Queen of England, because she is chock-full of social graces. Emily is the perfect combination of reverent and fun. She is like a human tulip—delicate and colorful. Katie is a spark plug, so full of life and fun and spontaneity. She took a day off work to take me to get a root canal, and afterward we had frozen drinks and Mexican food. I'm sure it has been documented in medical journals as The Greatest Root Canal Experience of All Time.

My girlfriends know me—really know me—and they have been my primary community in Nashville. We try hard to be honest about our sins. And when I seem to forget it, they take turns reminding me that I love Jesus and want to follow Him.

* * *

Each week at TNJC, we cook dinner while we catch up on each other's lives, then we gradually move into the living room, camping out on couches and over-stuffed pillows. We read the Bible and whatever book we're studying, and we pray through our hardships and laugh a lot. We talk about real-life stuff like relationships and jobs and fears and how God has something to say about all those things.

When TNJC started feeling like it came too infrequently, Amber began organizing breakfasts on Friday mornings so that we could have more time together. At seven o'clock, we meet at Frothy Monkey, an upscale coffee shop just down the street from my house. That pretty much kills me, because I usually don't go to sleep until at least three in the morning. It requires a great amount of commitment for me to haul my body out of bed at a quarter to seven and crawl down the block, but the girls are worth it.

Tonight at TNJC, Amber told me that it hurt her feelings when I told them that I was considering a move to New York City. "It's like you're saying that your friends there are better than your friends here," she said. She was right to feel hurt—even though that was not what I meant by it.

"All of our friends here are moving into a new phase of life," I told her. "And that's a natural shift, I know ... but I'm tired of feeling so alone here. You have a husband and coworkers that you see every day. Shannon and Jenny have those things. Katie and Emily have boyfriends and regular jobs, too. I don't have those things, and I can't expect you to fill that place in my life, either. You all have different priorities and I understand that, but three hours of friendship each week isn't enough for me."

I don't think it's okay for me to be alone all the time on the road and then be alone at home, too. I know that I've grown closer to God when I've been in the midst of community, and that I suffer when I'm not surrounded by people who encourage me. I love my friends in Nashville, but so many of them are married now, and they have less and less time for community. I can't force Nashville to be what it once was to me, and it doesn't seem willing to budge under the weight of my loneliness and longing for community. My need for that is more of a daily or semi-daily thing instead of a weekly thing, and I think maybe I need to be around other people who have similar needs.

I want so much for everyone to have a group of friends like the ones I have known in Nashville—for everyone to feel that kind of love and community. It was bright and tangibly beautiful while it lasted—when we were going out every Friday night and taking group vacations and spending holidays together as a giant makeshift family. But life has faded to a paler shade because of all the changes that are happening around me.

So I am lonely again, in a city that does not seem to fit me anymore. I have plenty of friends, but not the kind who have enough space in their lives to hang out a couple of times a week. Community is the most vital part of my decision about where to live. It is bigger than a job (especially since my job is mobile) or weather or cost of living, because it is the only one of those things that feeds my soul in any kind of eternal way. I want to deepen my roots in Nashville, but I can also feel something pulling at me, and I think it might be God calling me to put down roots in another city—where a whole new batch of strangers is waiting to be met, and where other friends are making room for me to drop anchor.

11

Half-Truths

I HOPE THAT MY THERAPIST is helping.

Her name is Rainey, and she's a smiling blond woman in her early forties. I've been seeing her for about six months now. On my first visit, she immediately set me at ease by offering me a bottle of water as soon as I walked into her office. Water is my Linus blanket. When I play shows, I request so much water from the venues that they usually think I'm either a band or a diabetic. I grabbed the bottle from Rainey and tried to relax against the arm of the couch. I had a bad case of cotton-mouth anyway. I hadn't felt nervousness like that in a long time, but I recognized it by the violent shaking of my leg and the fact that I had apparently just fallen off the nail-biting wagon.

She asked me to tell her about myself and why I was there. I fidgeted with the cap on the bottle. I spilled some facts about being a touring musician, and how that put additional stress on my relationships back home, how it made me work harder to maintain them, and how my efforts came across as pushy sometimes.

That was true, but only half true.

I took another sip of water, then I ponied up and said, "Okay, here's the deal—I think I have control issues. And I'm sure those are rooted in my fear of losing people, which is rooted in my lack of faith in God. And if I could just learn to trust Him more in my actual life, not just in my head, then I wouldn't be such a jerk to my friends sometimes. I'd stop grabbing at things and people. And then maybe they wouldn't go away."

The first thing that she said was, "Wow. You've self-diagnosed so much that you've saved yourself six months of counseling. It takes me a long time to get most people to that point."

I mentally patted myself on the back, because of course, I want to impress even my therapist. I wanted her to think I was so great that she'd try to set me up with one of her sons (if she had one). *I have this client*, she'd tell him. *She's just so wonderful and perfect for you, Steve* (which is what I named her imaginary son). It's ironic how I wanted this woman to think I had it all together, when we both knew that I was there because I had come to the conclusion that I *didn't* have it all together.

Rainey diagnosed me as "co-dependent." At the end of my first session, I asked her for a homework assignment. I am a task-oriented person, and I thought this might not only prompt me toward a quicker healing, but also have the added benefit of saving me thousands of dollars in counseling sessions. She told me to get a book called *Love Is a Choice*. I went out the next day and bought not only the book, but the workbook too.

* * *

My life has been defined primarily by the things I have lost (loved ones, opportunities, weight, etc.) and the one thing I can never lose (my salvation). That series of losses has trained me to regard my long-term relationships as somewhat-disposable investments. It bothers me that I have begun to expect them to end. But it's no exaggeration to say that every person whom I have ever called my "best friend" has suddenly left my life without warning. I pretty much keep that term out of my vocabulary now, with good reason: it is the kiss of death.

Somehow, nearly everyone I have cherished (outside of my family) has had about a two-year window in my life, and then—presto change-o—they're MIA. You can imagine that this has wreaked havoc on my relationship-esteem. It lends itself to a bit of self-loathing, which only serves to reassure me that I'm made to be left.

Psychologists—at least the ones on *Oprah*—say that every woman's greatest fear is abandonment. It rings true in my life. Part of the subconscious reason that I usually fall for missionary boys or other men of integrity is probably because, theoretically, a man of integrity will never leave me, have an affair, desire another woman besides me, fail, sin, hurt me, or forget my birthday.

In my most recent loss—a friendship with Harry—I did everything possible to ensure that he would stick around. He was my closest friend for nearly two years. It rapidly developed into one of those inappropriately close friendships that leaves onlookers wondering if one of the two, or maybe both, has feelings for the other.

I knew *everything* about Harry. I knew the sins that he told no one else about, I knew what time he woke up, I knew the scars across his body and how he got them, and I even knew when he "lusted." We talked at least once a day, sometimes more. Sometimes for hours.

I was at war with myself all along, trying to ignore the red flags, meanwhile settling into the easy flow of our friendship. I excused a lot of the inappropriate things about our situation because it meant so much to me that someone made the effort to be in touch with me every day. Most people do the hokey-pokey around me, based on whether or not I'm on tour—*You put your friendship in, you take your friendship out*—but with Harry, daily communication was a given. It felt like home. I knew it was a sorry excuse, but it's the one I let myself use.

* * *

Harry and I began to fight a lot in the last year of our friendship, in part because he started dating this girl who said she was a Christian but who never really exhibited anything indicative of that. He did all the necessary work to convince himself she really was a Christian, and he fed all of his friends the polished stories about her that would yield their approval. I'm sure I would've done the same thing if I were in his shoes. But because he was a bit more honest with me, I knew about the other side of his relationship with her. And I didn't hesitate to tell him that his church-hating, drug-addicted girlfriend was probably not, in fact, a Christian, especially given the statements she made about her spirituality.

I wasn't really in a position to judge him because I've dated my fair share of non-Christians—or perhaps that earned me an even better vantage point—but I could see him falling in love with her. I watched him drop his convictions for her, and then I watched him drop off the face of the earth when he began to spend every free moment with her. It wasn't the nonchalant, casual relationship that he had intended or led himself to believe he was capable of. And I was afraid for him. And I was afraid for me. And I am kind of outspoken about these things, to say the least.

So I started hinting around with subtle statements like "What, exactly, do you think you're doing?"

He would retaliate with one of two responses: "I didn't ask for your opinion on what girl I should date!" or "You're scripturally out of line for trying to tell me what to do, because women shouldn't hold men accountable!" Ad nauseam.

The fighting continued, even after they eventually broke up. Sometimes we fought over stupid things I said that made him feel judged; sometimes it was stupid things he said that offended me. Usually both—in the same conversation. That grew increasingly difficult for me, primarily because I was in love with him.

* * *

> *I liked everything about you,*
> *Except the way you treated me.*
> —DAVID WILCOX, "Distant Water"

A month after they broke up, Harry was still depressed and sad and spending all of his time secluded in his apartment in Los Angeles. One day when we were talking, he said he couldn't stand the loneliness and that he'd like it if I came for a visit. I could hear it in his voice—that devastation of losing someone you care about. The thought of him suffering alone was more than I could bear, even though his relationship with her is what started the demise of ours. I bought my ticket while we were still on the phone and flew out to see him two days later.

Since my trip happened to fall around the time of his birthday, I decided to throw him a surprise party at a hip Hollywood restaurant that he mentioned wanting to try. I was certain that would be a good way to cheer him up, and I couldn't wait to see the smile on his face. I planned and schemed and secretly invited all of his friends and paid the exorbitant rate for a birthday cake in Hollywood ($83). The night of the party, I managed to get him to the restaurant by convincing him that we were going to meet up with a business acquaintance of mine for dinner. He didn't seem the least bit suspicious—it was perfect!

When we walked in, he got the big "Happy Birthday," and he smiled and gushed about how thankful and surprised he was—and he really was! Yippee! Then he proceeded to step outside with everyone else in our party so they could smoke, because L.A. doesn't allow smoking in restaurants. Someone had to stay inside to hold the table and watch everyone's bags, and since I was the only nonsmoker, they all assumed it should be me. As I sat there alone, other patrons shuffled in and out of the busy restaurant, glaring at me for holding the largest table.

A middle-aged waiter came by carrying a tray of bowls and empty champagne glasses and said, "If you're dining alone tonight, could you move to a smaller table?"

"But I'm *not* alone. I'm with all of those people who are standing out on the sidewalk," I said. "I'm staying here to watch their bags and hold their seats."

I looked out of the window and saw them laughing and talking. I waited ... Ordered another drink. I watched the door. I scanned the menu ... Watched the door again.

Half an hour later they finally returned, laughing at the end of what was apparently the funniest story ever told. By then, I was furious. Or hurt. Or something. Not only did it never occur to him that I was inside *alone*, but it also never occurred to him to apologize after they returned. I struggled to keep my cool, especially after all I'd done to fly out and put the event together, because I didn't want to be a jerk in front of his friends. The truth is, I was cursing him in my head.

Later, he asked me to take a picture of him with all of his friends at the party. Unsure of what I'd done to deserve exclusion from the photo, I imagined smashing the cake over his head and leaving the restaurant, never to return.

I would be remiss not to mention that he is extremely courteous to most people. He is the kind of guy who will offer you his coat before you even mention that you're cold. So this behavior was totally atypical, and it came across as especially hurtful since it seemed to be directed specifically at me. And also because of the being in love with him thing.

* * *

When you love someone who doesn't love you back, it is the most devastating experience of all. It's tempting to try too hard to make it work. It's tempting to push. I'm sure I did both of those things as time wore on.

And Harry pushed back with abrasive statements that ripped my lungs out. One night we were talking about how I had lost some weight since I had started running and, like any girl, was excited about losing more. He said, "I think you're fine the way you are." I was elated! Until he followed it with, "It really doesn't make a difference if you lose more weight or not. The problem is that you're *tall*, and guys like petite girls."

Devastated, I cursed the five-foot-eight frame that I'd been happy with only moments earlier. It cut to the core. My pain didn't come so much from the fact that he didn't love me, as from the way he went about not loving me—like he was intentionally adding insult to injury.

Sometimes your words are thick as lead
You swing them strong upside my head.
—DAVE BARNES, "Sticks & Stones"

Then things got weirder. Somewhere in the midst of all our fighting, he kissed me. And I kissed him back. Our relationship deteriorated even further into a mangled mess of bipolarity: fighting, then kissing, then fighting again. All along, he knew where my heart was, though I never admitted it. Loving him didn't fit into words. It was bigger than Antonio. Bigger than my history. Bigger than the sins we committed against each other.

I didn't want to call things off because, after all, he was the only guy I'd ever kissed that I also loved. Sometimes I tried to date other guys, to move toward something healthy. It didn't work very well. Once he even called and yelled at me when he found out I was with another guy. It was so confusing and only fed my hope that he might love me someday.

At least once a month, he asked out random girls and called me at the end of every date to report on how it had gone. Strangers, all of them—beautiful, petite strangers with long, straight blond hair. I had learned to be mostly at peace with my appearance, but his actions screamed that I was not good enough to love. Only good enough to talk to every day and share his most intimate secrets with. Good enough to use as a stand-in girlfriend until something better came along. But he did not want to be with me. It felt like he was too proud to love me back; I was not his Texas beauty queen.

You can't force-feed love down the throat of a man
Who is dying for affection,
And you can't turn the head of a man
Whose face is always looking in the other direction.
—ARIANA TERRELL, "Humpty Dumpty"

12

When Harry Left Sally

ONE NIGHT WHEN I WAS ON TOUR in Austin, I opened my laptop and saw an email from Harry with a subject line that said: "Thoughts." When I opened it and saw the length of it, I knew something was up. His emails were always short and to-the-point; this one was longer than one page.

I read his words: *Effective immediately, I think we should cease all contact. I can't do this anymore. I don't think our friendship is in line with God's plan ...*

Surely someone had poured acid into my lungs—that was the only possible explanation for the indescribable sensation I had. I read the email three times before I could even process it. I alternated between wrenching pain and seething anger.

Less than a month earlier, I had tried to bring closure to our relationship, and he had pleaded with me not to walk away. He had built an imaginary fence behind me and another fence in front of me, hemming me in so that I could not get to him but could not get away. Then, when he finally had the upper hand, he played the "God Card," which came across more like a power play than anything. It seemed contrived because, unlike Antonio, it didn't measure up with the rest of his lifestyle.

It was just another dent in my hopes that someday, somewhere ... someone will stay.

It is hardest to be left by someone who knows you well, because they are leaving the real you. And Harry knew me better than anyone. For nearly two years, we shared every detailed story with each other—from the pointless minutiae of our days to the secrets that had never been exposed to the light. It was too much, and I knew it all along. When he left, I felt like I was being ripped in two by some unseen force that I was helpless to fight.

Honestly, he was no villain. I began to take my share of the blame for the way our friendship fell apart. And I began to blame myself for the way a lot of my friendships have fallen apart. So when I began to recognize this pattern of lost relationships, I started seeing Rainey to figure out exactly what it was that made me push people away.

* * *

I was on tour in Texas with my friend Paul, whom I refer to as Sarcastic Paul, when I first considered seeing a therapist. I had a good friend back in Nashville who had been seeing Rainey for close to a year and loved her. I paced the worn carpet in the green room at the venue in Beaumont, trying to decide whether or not to make the call.

"Do you think I should see a therapist or a counselor or something to deal with this Harry stuff?" I asked Sarcastic Paul.

"*Nooooo*, of course not," he said.

I took the hint and quietly made the call, hoping no one over-heard me leaving the message. "Um ... I'm looking into starting therapy, and I'd love to know if you have any openings. *Soon.*" I was ashamed that I needed to see a therapist, but I was eager to get there, nonetheless.

I had this notion of what my first meeting would be like—how I would walk in and announce that I knew exactly what my problem was, and we'd celebrate my wisdom and discernment over a glass of Pellegrino, and then I'd be on my merry way, fully restored!

And I really *did* know what my problem was. But I didn't have a clue how to start solving it.

Actually, I kind of did, to be honest. I knew the big picture; it was just the baby steps that baffled me. I briefly saw a counselor in high school, when I lost a friend to suicide. It sped the heal-ing in so many ways, but the main thing that I remember is that everything started to come together when I got things straight in my relationship with Jesus. When I started therapy back then, I was dealing with some boy issues on top of my friend's suicide, and those two things were the dominant topics. Six months later, I remember sitting in my therapist's office and telling him how it broke my heart that I knew people in my European history class who were hurting and struggling, and how I wanted so desperately to show them God's love.

It's strange how the healing comes to that. But it does. Healing comes when you're closer to the Healer.

So I guess I knew that I needed to get things straight with Jesus. I knew that I needed to trust Him more, to believe that God isn't holding out on me. Because it's that very subconscious belief that prompts me to grab at things, to try to control things.

I did that a lot with Harry, probably more than in any other relationship I've ever had. So I could see why that would push a person away, but I couldn't stop doing it, no matter how hard I tried. I ached for him to see something worth loving in me—intelligence or wit or kindness to people—the very thing that he said he was searching for in all those tiny, blond strangers. And he acknowledged that he saw those things in me, but he never found them worth loving. I kept struggling to be someone he thought was good enough for his love, instead of trusting God with my heart and my future.

I heard someone smart share a great metaphor about how hell is a place where all the pots are boiling over and all the milk is spoiled—and the man's job is to do something about it, and the woman's job is to do *nothing* about it. Women tend to want to control things. But the more I learn to trust God to be in control, the less pressing the need is to handle things myself.

* * *

It was obvious to me that I was not so close to God at that point. And in the months since Harry ended our friendship, I've been trying to get closer to Him again. I started trying to pray again a few months ago, and it's been an interesting path. Every time I try to start talking to God again, it mostly begins the way it does when you try to rekindle a relationship with an estranged friend. First, you do small talk, the catching up. Then, after a few attempts, you can work into a deeper conversation.

> *My Bible is like a roommate who ain't talking,*
> *Or maybe it's me who's been keeping to myself.*
> —WAITING FOR DECEMBER, "California"

My small talk with God consists mainly of my asking Him for things that I want. I tend to forget that I'm supposed to do other things, like thank Him, praise Him, and confess my sins. I might do a little intercession, but that's basically just asking for things that I want, but for *other* people. Nonetheless, I hope it constitutes a start. And I think after a while, I'll begin to talk to God about other things again, the deeper things. I want that a lot. I guess maybe I should ask for *that.*

Today, I thanked Him for my food at one meal, asked Him to help me know whether or not to move to New York City, asked Him to keep me safe on my four-hour drive to the venue tonight, and begged Him to prompt The Boy I'm Starting to Like to call me.

Maybe next week I'll start confessing my lust and my pride and my vanity. I'll confess that I am jealous of the body (and the shoes) of the girl who was in line in front of me at the grocery store. I'll confess that I still harbor anger and even hatred toward Harry for the way he treated me. And I'll confess that right now I care far too little about the lost and hurting people in the world ... not nearly as much as I did when I was a fresh-faced seventeen-year-old in European history.

I hope that someday I will stop hating Harry and that my heart will grow past all the pain of messing things up and being scared and being treated the worst by the one I've loved the most. I hope that I will trust God more and talk to Him about other things besides how I wish the phone would ring and it would be The Boy. I hope that I will care about the lost and the orphans and the widows, and stop being so self-centered.

Wish me faith.

13

Highway Miles
—Exit 2

Pennsylvania: March 2003

DEREK WEBB WAS "BOASTING NO MORE" on the
Caedmon's Call CD in my car when at least one of my four wheels
left the ground. I thought I'd hit an animal, maybe a large dog or a
llama. Whatever it was, it left my car riding terribly roughly when
I returned to the ground. *Thump thump thump.* "No more, my God
..." Derek sang.

I pulled over to the shoulder of the four-lane Pennsylvania
highway. The only thing I knew for sure was that I had a flat tire on
the front driver's side. I could tell by the way the car was pulling
violently to the left and leaning ever so much toward the ground
on that side. I stepped out into the cold rain to see if there was any
damage to the body of the car, but it all seemed clear. As I was
reaching into the car for my cell phone to call AAA, I stopped

short, because a red SUV was pulling up in front of me.

At first I thought they were just coming to my aid, but then I noticed that they shared that familiar *thump thump thump* sound. The red SUV was another victim of the highway. They came back to see if I was okay. I went back again to grab my phone and call AAA, when we saw yet another car pulling in behind us. *Thump thump thump.*

"Any idea what that thing actually was?" I asked the people from the SUV.

"It was just a huge, sharp rock in the road. It must've fallen off the mountain," one of them replied.

"We should move it before it gets anyone else. It's already taken out three of us," another guy suggested.

After some assessing, we realized that we each had a spare tire. However, I was the only one without some knowledge of how to actually *use* it. They started replacing their tires while I sat in the dark on the side of Route 15 at 7:34 p.m. I figured I should call AAA since it looked like I was alone in my plight. When I got through to the operator, he informed me that he wouldn't be able to dispatch anyone because the system was down temporarily.

But without hesitation or complaint, Anne and Robbie (from the SUV) as well as Gary and Eric (from the car) came over to change my tire for me. Robbie was lying on the ground in the rain, jacking up my Camry. Gary held the flashlight. Anne held the lug nuts and helped Robbie with the tire. Eric watched for traffic. I was standing idly by, saying "thank you" frequently. Did I mention that Gary and Eric missed a concert (Disturbed and Seville) to stick around and help me?

At the end of our long, unexpected bonding experience, all I had to offer each of them was a copy of my CD. That didn't seem like quite enough. These strangers had gone to bat for me. They had sacrificed their time and comfort—in the rain and the cold—to change the tire of a girl who should've learned how to do it for herself a long time ago.

It was an encouraging experience for me, though. I ended up thanking God for my flat tire ... thanking Him for the opportunity to have some strangers restore my faith in humanity ... thanking Him for providing for me in the midst of my trouble ... thanking Him for keeping us all safe there on the side of the road while the eighteen-wheelers roared past us.

When I cranked my ignition, Cliff Young started singing about how "the Lord is a Warrior ... the Lord is a Deliverer of those who put their trust in Him." And I sat there with my wet hair and clothes, shivering from the cold, singing in agreement, and wearing a smile that I couldn't restrain.

* * *

Boise, Idaho: August 2003

The Federal Aviation Administration sure did a number on touring musicians. We're not allowed to carry guitars onboard anymore (and a big thanks to United for beating up my guitar *twice*). It also dropped the weight limit of checked luggage from seventy pounds to fifty pounds. My roommates and I spent most of the night before my flight to Boise trying to reduce my luggage to the appropriate sizes and weights. Here's the breakdown:

Carryon 1: 15" x 9" x 21"—This small bag must hold all of my clothes, shoes, toiletries, hair dryer, pillow, Bible, journal, books, etc.

Carryon 2: Purse/laptop bag.

Checked Luggage 1: Guitar.

Checked Luggage 2: This is a suitcase where I carry all my merchandise and gear, stacks of CDs, T-shirts, stickers, guitar cables, strings, pedal boxes, microphones. It is incredibly difficult for this stuff to weigh less than fifty pounds. CDs alone are pretty heavy, and hauling gear is no picnic.

If you want to travel with more luggage than the allotted amount, you have to pay extra. Where, exactly, this money would come from is anyone's guess.

Just in time for my flight, I finally figured out the exact outfit that I could wear in order to get through security without being stopped for buttons, zippers, hair clips, or whatever. The outfit included a T-shirt that I made myself, which says "I (heart) THE NRA" across the front.

I joined the National Rifle Association a few years ago after I spent a year as a vegan. In an attempt to get some healthy food while on tour (instead of the typical lasagna, spaghetti, or pizza that most venues provide), I forced myself into the land of no meat and no dairy. It didn't really work. At all. The carbs wreaked havoc on my system, causing me to gain nearly twenty pounds that year, so I opted to quit being a vegan and went back to eating meat and milk products. Except my body couldn't handle meat anymore. Finally, my friend Jackson suggested that I try some of the venison left over from his last hunting season, and I was so happy that I was able to eat it—no preservatives, no steroids, and it tasted like heaven.

"This is incredible," I said. "Where can I get more of this? I've never seen it in grocery stores."

"In Tennessee, it's illegal to sell wild game like venison, so you have to hunt it yourself," he told me.

And that is how I went from being a vegan to being a hunter in a matter of seconds. To top off the experience, I joined the NRA. Jackson shed tears of joy as I signed the papers.

As I walked through the Nashville airport, people smiled and laughed when they saw me wearing my NRA shirt. So I was taken aback during my layover at Chicago O'Hare when people responded with nervousness and hostility. But then, on my flight from Chicago to Boise, a man high-fived me—without a word—as I walked to my seat.

It wasn't long before I realized that I was seated in what can only be described as the Worst Possible Seat Ever. Crying baby in the row behind me? Check. Baby's older sibling kicking my seat repeatedly? Check. Entirely oblivious parent? Yep. Plus, I was in the middle of the row, packed in between a drunk priest (on the aisle) and an eight-year-old girl who was traveling alone (on the window). I was operating on about thirty-seven minutes of sleep, since I had stayed up all night trying to get my luggage down to the acceptable weight, and I wasn't really in the mood for a three-hour flight. The little girl was on some kind of hyperactivity-inducing medication. The priest was on some kind of I-hate-everyone-and-everything medication. I think he slipped some of it in my decaf.

I put in my earplugs, donned my eye mask, and tried to sleep. At the exact moment that I finally drifted off, the little girl decided she needed to use the lavatory. Of course. I felt bad for being frustrated with her, because she was a sweet little thing. But seriously ... *thirty-seven minutes of sleep.*

I arrived in Boise and was waiting for my luggage when two guys came up to me. One of them wore a shirt with Elmer Fudd on the front. Emblazoned above Elmer's head were the words "Wabbit Hunter." He was also holding a sign that had my picture and my name on it. He had drawn a halo around my head and given me angel wings.

Stephen ("Wabbit Hunter") and his friend Dan carried my luggage and helped me take my guitar over to United's customer relations desk to complain that they had, once again, beaten the crap out of it. Despite the fact that it had a nice little sticker on it that said "Inspected—OK," it was *not*, in fact, "OK." Here we go again.

We began the two-hour trek to Twin Falls, and I was getting along just dandy with Stephen and Dan because we liked the same music, and we talked for a long time about hunting. Then Stephen told me he had been worried that I might be pretentious or rude, since I was a "big-time Nashville musician" (his words, not mine). But he said that the moment he saw my NRA T-shirt, he knew we'd be friends for a long time.

I was in Idaho to play a festival in Twin Falls called Rock the Canyon at Snake River Canyon. You may remember that canyon as the place where Evel Knievel attempted to jump his motorcycle/skycycle in 1974. Granted, I wasn't even close to being alive then, but having grown up in a motorcycle-loving family, I knew all about it. From the time I got my first motorcycle at age five, I dreamed of marrying him (this was pre-Kirk Cameron, mind you). I *had* to see the spot where he began the jump. The mound is located on private property, so we were very discreet when we snuck onto the land to take pictures of it.

The promoters of the RTC festival were amazing people, and they arranged to have three sweet RVs for the artists to stay in while we waited to go onstage during the assaulting heat. My set was at 5:30 p.m. on Friday. That is the hottest time of the day, according to locals. And I'll fill you in on a little secret: there is no way that a guitar player can wear shorts on stage without looking like an idiot, unless he's Angus Young or a member of the Red Hot Chili Peppers. Which, by the way, I am not. So I had to wear jeans, and the only jeans I had brought with me were black.

I stood onstage in my black jeans, holding my guitar in the 105-degree heat, with the sun beating directly down on me. I was super sweaty. In fact, there were times that my guitar strings became so hot that they burned my fingers when I touched them.

I had a good time hanging out with some of the other artists and doing some sightseeing in Twin Falls (*"Look! It's a waterfall! Oh, and there's another one just like it!"*). Mostly, we hung out in the RV and traded road stories. It was so good not to be alone again for once. And it was that trip that helped forge my friendship with Stephen, which continues to this day. Some of my favorite people in the world are people I've met on the road. In fact, a few of them are the reason I moved to Nashville, because they lived there and made it seem like it could be a good home for me.

Two years after I met Stephen, he moved to Nashville, too. When I picked him up at the airport, he said, "You know, I never thought my life would change this much just because of some T-shirt."

* * *

Asheville, North Carolina: September 2003

I remember unpacking my things in an amazing hotel in the mountains of Asheville. I recall it distinctly because it was the biggest hotel room I had ever stayed in, and also because it was only my second time ordering room service. For the record, my first time ordering room service didn't really count; I only ordered it because I was alone in Colorado Springs and was too sick to leave my room. I could've died alone in my hotel room, clinging to the wafer-thin pillow, so the room service was more of a last resort than a luxury.

In Asheville, I ordered the continental breakfast, which included coffee, fruit, and a poppy-seed muffin. It didn't cost me anything because the college where I was playing graciously set up an expense account for me.

As I drove back from the show later that night, I looked across the street from my hotel and saw war veterans crowded outside a shelter. It occurred to me, momentarily, how very wrong this seemed. *They fight for our country—they get to sleep and eat in a shelter. I sing a few songs on a stage—I get a posh hotel room and room service*. It's something I don't know how to reconcile.

The college put me up there for two nights, and I hardly knew what to do with myself. Mostly, there was a lot of dancing around in front of the mirror while wearing the white cotton robe from the bathroom. The only things missing were Richard Gere, a red dress, a diamond necklace, and some scary hooker boots. I rarely get put up in nice places, and I never, *ever* get an unlimited expense account. I'm accustomed to $.59 Exxon coffee, not room service. I'm not used to a room with a view of the mountains. I'm not used to having a Pfister faucet in my shower.

Days like that, it's easy to be a musician. It's easy to sit back in my king-sized bed and forget about all the nights I spent in the Motel 6, trying to ignore the smell of stale smoke and praying that no one would break into my room.

But just a few days after that, I was at home, trying to write the music for the next album. As usual, I sat there for hours, praying that something—anything—would come to me. That is the real work for me. Words come easy, but music is the struggle. I hit the same wall every time. For some reason, that's what I kept dreading as I sat there staring out at the Appalachians from my hotel room.

I have a way with things like that ... a way of ruining the perfect with thoughts of the pending. For instance, thoughts of the fall and winter always seem to leave a stain on the last few weeks of summer. The leaves were green as I stared out of my window that day, but they were threatening to change. The change itself is pretty, but far too temporary. When all the color starts receding, people make happy eyes and bright statements like "Oh, I just love the chill in the air!" I, on the other hand, secretly wish them frostbite.

It's not that I don't like fall; I do. My only problem with fall is that it lives right next door to winter. And winter ... *boo!* Not a fan. Coats are cumbersome. Pant legs never dry. Give me the hot, hot heat of Tucson. Give me that again, *please!* Melt my skin.

I'm sure I should probably say something meaningful about how I'm trying to be content, no matter what my circumstances. But I'll save that statement for summer. Right now, I'm sitting outside a café in Chicago, and I need a jacket.

* * *

New York, New York: May 2005

Manhattan was still quite cold at night even though it was early May. Spring hadn't fully set in, and the April rain lingered. I settled into the City for a week to play shows and hang out with friends. Wednesday night was an off-night for me, so my friend Tom and I decided to see a movie and grab some dinner in Midtown.

I found an empty parking spot on West Forty-fourth Street, a few blocks from the theater, and walked over to meet Tom at the ticket booth. After we survived the latest Ashton Kutcher disaster,

I walked back to West Forty-fourth, and my car was nowhere to be seen. Nowhere. I started to panic—*Did I park at a different inter-section? Has my car been towed? Or worse yet, has it been stolen and sold for parts at some gritty chop shop, like in the movies?*

I flagged down a police officer, who informed me that my car had, in fact, been towed. Apparently the "No Standing" sign nearby really meant "No Parking." Silly me. I thought it meant "no standing," as in, "You can't stand here." As in, "We've had too many people standing in the street while trying to hail cabs, and some of them (especially stupid Southerners like you) have been getting hit by cars, so please stay on the sidewalk and don't stand in the street."

My car had been towed to a dock in Hell's Kitchen. The cop graciously agreed to give us a ride to the dock since it was raining and windy and my coat was in the trunk of my car. When we got there, we waited in line for nearly an hour, until they finally called my name. I stepped up, excited to redeem my car, "Trigger," from the mouth of the Hudson River.

The lady behind the counter—we'll call her Marge—was none too happy to see me. My out-of-state license gave her even more of a reason to spread on an extra layer of bitterness. I handed her my credit card, grateful that this would all be over soon.

"Cash only. Read the sign," Marge said, in a well-practiced string of words, delivered in monotone.

"Excuse me?" I asked sincerely, because I hadn't understood what she said.

"*Read* the sign," Marge said emphatically. This time her words were paced and heavy and suggested that she wanted to stab me in the eye with her letter opener.

The sign was *behind* her, so I hadn't been able to see it until I stepped up to the counter. Sure enough, there on the cream-colored cinderblock walls, in small lettering just below the smear of blood (which surely belonged to some other fool who dared to cross Marge), I saw the words "Cash Only."

"Do you have an ATM?" I asked.

"Do you *see* an ATM?" she responded as she stretched her arm out and swept her hand across the landscape of the room with overt sarcasm.

"All right, then," I said. "Where is the nearest ATM?"

"Four blocks north, at the Circle Line."

Tom and I braced ourselves for the wind and rain, then stepped out into the night again. By this time it was after one in the morning. We walked to the ATM as I griped about how I had enough cash in the car to pay the impound fee, if only they'd let me *into* my car.

We made it back safely to the impound lot, stood in line again, and I handed my cash to Marge. She pointed down a dark corridor and said sharply, "Go."

After Tom and I crossed the narrow walkway to get to my car, he pointed out that there was a parking ticket on my windshield. It was $115, in addition to the impound fee! All for "standing." As it turns out, a "No Standing" violation is one of the most severe parking violations you can get. Marge told me it's worse than parking in front of a hydrant or a "No Parking" sign. Apparently "No Standing" means "Do not even stop here—not even for a second. Don't even wonder what it might be like to slow down within a three-block radius of this spot, or we will rip the money from your pockets with a force greater than the rage of Mike Tyson on steroids."

I went to pay the ticket a few weeks after I returned home, and it was then that I stumbled upon an even more astonishing thing—I realized that there was not just *one* parking ticket, but *two*. The rain had caused them to stick together. Seriously? Two parking tickets in three hours? A little hyperactive, aren't we, Captain Parking Ticket? Perhaps the NYC DOT needs to lay off the C-R-A-C-K.

Fortunately, I made enough money on the tour to cover the tickets. *Unfortunately*, in a flash—like Marge's patience—it was gone.

14

Texas

Lubbock, Texas: February 2003

TOUR GUS. That's what we named the fifteen-passenger van
that we toured in that month. If you say it out loud, it sounds kind
of like "Tour Bus," which is what we were shooting for. I have
a serious case of Tour Bus Lust whenever we pass a big Prevost
on the highway, so I was trying to get as close as I could to that. I
wrote a cheesy poem about my Tour Bus Lust one day when we
passed a row of them heading into Austin:

"Prevost"
—TARA LEIGH COBBLE

Leather and chrome
And you roll on by
You're a mile long

> *And a mountain high*
> *He's dreaming—*
> *Safe, up in his bunk*
> *While I sleep with the blanket*
> *From my trunk*
> *And you are the dream*
> *I dream the most*
> *Shiny, beautiful*
> *Prevost.*

We packed Tour Gus with four people, six guitars, and a charangua (some kind of Argentinean instrument), plus one and a half flats of bottled water. We also had the sound system, a boatload of merchandise, and whatever luggage we could carry.

My tourmates on that trip were:

John Delony—a newlywed guy who shares my sense of humor. His personality and appearance are akin to Johnny Knoxville. Always a prankster. He's a "what you see is what you get" kind of guy, and I like that just fine. We called him "D-Lo."

Eric Peters—the guy who brought the charangua. Eric initially comes off a little on the non-conversational side, but he has a delayed personality that is just hiding behind all of that. He has a knack for writing songs that stick in your head for days on end. Late at night, I lay in bed with his melodies on repeat in my brain.

Danielle Peters—Eric's lovely wife and our tour manager. She's a pretty little thing who can beat the merch table into submission with one flash of her eye. She knitted in the van during most of the drives. And she was the one to offer words of encouragement every night when we played the delightful game of "Post-Show Pro/Con."

In Post-Show Pro/Con, we told each other what we did right and wrong during the show that night. It was supposed to help us improve our craft, but we mostly used it to berate and belittle each other.

"You talked too much," Eric would tell me.

"Yeah, well at least I know how to *speak*, Silent Bob!" I would retaliate.

"Your mom!" John would pipe up. "*Both* of your moms!"

Then he would hit the brakes and send us all hurtling toward the front of Tour Gus while he laughed at his little prank.

*   *   *

We played a mixed bag of colleges, churches, and coffee shops on the tour. After a few months of touring, we learned to anticipate what the venues would look like when we got there. We imagined them aloud as we drove there, offering up our best guesses of what awaited us.

Youth rooms are the most easily predictable—they tend to be named things like "The Fire Escape" or, if they have a coffee machine, "Common Grounds." They're usually painted graffiti-style with all colors of spray paint and cluttered with random "stolen" street signs. If street signs are present, you can guarantee there will be a "One Way" sign pointing toward heaven. And if you're lucky, the youth group room will also have games like foosball and ping-pong.

The night of our first show, I had to drag Eric and John away from the game tables to play the concert. That was the beginning of their incredibly competitive ping-pong tournament, which reared its ugly head at nearly every venue thereafter. Eric spanks at ping-pong, and that's how John ended up losing the T-shirt bet.

Somehow we had gotten our hands on this T-shirt that was straight out of church camp. It was navy and had large yellow block lettering across the front that said "ASK ME ABOUT JESUS CHRIST, MY PERSONAL LORD AND SAVIOR." The words covered the *entire* front of the shirt.

We were nearing an all-out war over who would have to wear this shirt on a given night of the tour. It all came down to The Texas Tour Ping-Pong Championship Finals of 2003, and John got smoked. So he had to wear the shirt at the venue of my choice. I thought Austin would be good, because the shirt would be the most ironic in that city. After all, the city's motto is "Keep Austin Weird," not "Keep Austin Churchy." But then I decided that Tour Gus might get his tires slit if John wore the shirt there. I didn't want to put Tour Gus in harm's way like that, so I assigned John the task of wearing it at a show in Lubbock, his old college town. He suffered a lot of ridicule from his college buddies. It was awesome. I have pictures.

* * *

San Antonio, Texas: February 2003

Tour Gus coasted into San Antonio one chilly afternoon late in the tour. We were a little worried because we didn't have a place to spend the night. The venue that night was a small place by the water, and their part of the deal did not involve providing accommodations for us.

I almost always prefer a hotel room—even a crappy one—to staying in someone's home because hotel rooms are familiar to me now. While Eric drove us into the city, John read aloud from an article about B.B. King, who had just built a new home for himself. According to the article, he had his bedroom designed to look like a hotel room so it would feel like home. We all nodded and raised our eyebrows as if to say, "Sadly, that makes total sense."

There's something to be said for personal space. I like to unpack my things at night, stand my cleanser and moisturizer up on the bathroom counter, use my own pillow—that way, it doesn't feel like I'm living out of a suitcase. But when you're on tour with other people, you trade the joy of personal space for the joy of company. Most nights, the four of us ended up sleeping at people's homes, sometimes in the same room.

I've spent nights in every imaginable location. During the early years of touring, I took a tent and sleeping bag with me because the venues weren't putting me up and I definitely couldn't afford it myself. Since then, I've stayed in everything from five-star hotel rooms to the front seat of my car, so I usually don't worry about it too much. Once, a promoter told me that he couldn't afford to put me up in a hotel but that I could have my pick of the top or bottom bunk in his seven-year-old daughter's bedroom. I didn't want to seem like an ingrate, but I was exhausted that night, so I took $40 out of my own pocket and got a room at Motel 6. When there are four people involved, however, it changes the decision-making process.

As we drove around town, we tried to recall if we knew anyone who lived in San Antonio that we could crash with. We were drawing a blank. The tour had been stacked with so many bizarre experiences by that time that we had started to refer to it as the "You've Gotta Be Freaking Kidding Me Tour." In fact, one night we played a show where our payment came not in the form of cash, but in cases of bottled water. We joked about sending them in to our landlords and utility companies in lieu of checks, since they were apparently a new form of currency.

We continued to rack our brains for potential housing options, but when nothing came to mind, we started to imagine sleeping in the van in the freezing Texas night.

"Just another thing to add to our list of weirdness," John said.

"Wait!" Eric said, excited to have uncovered a possible solution. "I know a girl who used to date a guy who moved to San Antonio!"

"Get her on the line and see if we can get his number!" John ordered.

In this type of scenario, it's nearly impossible not to feel like a dirtbag. Scrounging up numbers from third-degree strangers just to have a floor to sleep on? Welcome to life on the road.

Eric called her, and within minutes, we had our place to stay that night.

The guy—whom I'll call Bobby, but whose real name I cannot recall—was one of the kindest people I've ever met. He worked third shift at a restaurant in the city. I imagined his perplexity as Eric explained the situation to him over the phone: "So, Bobby, I'm friends with your ex-girlfriend, who gave me your number. I'm a musician, and I'm on tour with three of my friends, and we don't have a place to stay tonight. Do you have room for the four of us at your place?"

"Sure!" Bobby said. "I'm at the restaurant right now. Just swing by and I'll give you the key!"

Sweet Bobby. Brave Bobby.

We picked up the key and headed straight to the venue. After the show, we didn't stick around long because we were so tired from the drive that day. We closed up shop around midnight and headed back to Bobby's place.

It's hard to describe the reaction one might have when entering an apartment like Bobby's. It wasn't so much fear as it was shock—like the way you'd respond if you saw Charles Manson shopping at Hello Kitty. It was just an unusual sight to behold. Our eyes widened when we entered. The scene: floor-to-ceiling Star Wars. There was hardly a surface that was not covered in Yoda, Luke, or Darth. There were even Star Wars sheets on his bed.

The tiny bathroom was unbearably filthy, even by a man's standards. Eric and John refused to enter it. The interior of the toilet bowl was *orange*. Danielle and I began to clean it, not only for our sake but for Bobby's. After we got ready for bed, we divvied up the sleeping spaces. Danielle and Eric, the married couple, earned the bed without debate. John agreed to take a Princess Leia sleeping bag and sleep on the floor beside the bed. I got the spare sheets, which featured Chewy, and headed for the couch. It was like sleeping in a Star Wars museum.

At four in the morning, I awoke to John's rustling in the next room. Apparently the part of the floor he was sleeping on was directly below the window-mounted air conditioner. Not only had water been dripping on his head, but it had been dripping on the carpet for months prior to that, accumulating into a nice moldy scene. John moved to another part of the room, and I heard him start snoring again shortly after that. This was a good sign, considering he had to drive the next day.

When six thirty rolled around, Bobby knocked on the front door. He had given us his only key, so I had been assigned the task of letting him in when he got home from work. Bleary-eyed, I greeted him and went back to the couch immediately.

"Do you mind if I watch some TV before I go to bed?" he asked.

"Of course not, Bobby ... this is *your* home! Do whatever you want! Besides, I'm so tired that I'm sure I'll fall right back to sleep."

And I'm not kidding when I say that he turned on the television, leaned up against the couch where I was lying, and immediately started watching *Star Wars*. It was already in the DVD player. I couldn't help but think, *Is this what he does every morning after work? Is this his routine?*

I drifted back to sleep soon after. When I woke, Bobby was gone. My tourmates were up and dressed, getting ready to leave. We started to wonder if Bobby really existed or if it was all some strange dream. Just in case he *did* exist, we left him some cookies and a thank-you note that read:

Dear Bobby,

For letting us stay here, thank you we do. Gracious to strangers, you have been. You are wiser than Yoda and kinder than Princess Leia.

May the force be with you,

Eric, Danielle, John, and Tara Leigh

Danielle and I worried that he might think we were making fun of him with our own brand of Yoda-speak. John and Eric reasoned that we were just meeting him in his comfort zone.

Occasionally when I'm on tour, I run into interesting people like Bobby. As perplexed as I might've been by his décor, I envied his generosity. I don't know many people who would hand over their house key to four strange musicians. He gave up his bed and his privacy for us. How is it that someone can show that much kindness, and I can just soak it all up, offering only cookies in return?

* * *

Fort Worth, Texas: August 2004

I never know anyone at the party
And I'm always the host.
—COUNTING CROWS, "Mrs. Potter's Lullaby"

There are still days—even though I've done this for years—when this job breaks my will. As deep as my love for Texas is, I would've given anything to be anywhere else at the time. I drove west from Dallas to play at a church venue with a coffee lounge in the back. Prior to that night, I'd never set foot on Fort Worth soil, but I still had high hopes of a good turnout. Or any turnout at all.

I've noticed how much the size of the crowd affects the way they perceive me, and it discourages me sometimes. If I put on the exact same show for a small crowd and a large crowd, the small crowd will not think I'm as great, and they will not rave about the show to their friends afterward. There's some kind of subliminal thing that can make us all believe it's a better show if there are more people laughing and applauding.

That night, I tried desperately to win over the eight people in the room. From the heat of the spotlight, I turned the question over in my head a million times: *What do they need? I don't know these people ... I don't know their struggles and their joys. What can I give them that will last?* More than once, the whirring cappuccino machine in the back interrupted my train of thought—usually during the slow, pensive songs. Of course. I felt so helpless.

The singles pastor had already lectured me about the money situation—they weren't charging admission or trying to recoup their expenses, but he wanted a large turnout. They would've been able to get a "big-name artist" for just a little more money, he told me. I remember thinking, *If you're not trying to make money, then why does it matter? What makes a big-name artist's show more valid than mine? Numbers? Is that how I'm supposed to measure my worth? If so, then I'm a miserable failure.*

Words were coming out of my mouth as I sang, but my brain was spinning in a different direction, trying to tell myself to get over my personal misery and just love these people. Only two of them would even look me in the eye. I felt like I was getting nowhere. I prayed silently, *God, I need You to help me remember why I do this. Please remind me ... Do Something."*

I finished my set, but not without questioning myself a dozen more times and offering up at least as many prayers. After the show, one of the guys who wouldn't even look at me told me stories of his depression, his loneliness. He said that one of the songs that I sang really struck a chord of hope with him. Then he smiled.

And just like that, I remembered.

15

Rolling Up the Red Carpet

MY DAD WORRIES ABOUT ME being alone on the road so much, about all the driving through the night in a car that is more than a decade old. Last year, I joined AAA to appease him, but he still makes me carry flares in my trunk. Who *does* that?

He has also strongly suggested that I purchase the following safety items: blind-spot mirrors, fire extinguisher, stun gun, emergency hammer (to break out my window in case my car is suddenly submerged in water), pepper spray, first-aid kit, knife (to cut my seatbelt in case I am trapped), conceal carry permit (and all that it entails), Fix-A-Flat, new Rand McNally atlas every year ("They build new roads, you know"), and one of those large orange reflective triangles that truckers put up behind their trucks when they're parked on the side of the road. As a result, I now carry enough safety equipment to ensure that I would sink straight to the bottom of Lake Michigan should I ever encounter it, emergency hammer notwithstanding.

A few years ago, somewhere near Bloomington, Indiana, my faithful Camry traveled its 200,000th mile. That meant I had driven the equivalent of eight times the distance around the world in that car. I'm edging in on half a million miles now. And all that in just six years. The coolest part is my 200,000th mile took place near the hometown of one of the musicians who has most influenced me: John Cougar Mellencamp. Forgive me if I leave the "Cougar" in there, but it's a throwback to the '80s and I like it that way.

Right now I'm writing at Fido, a hip coffee shop in Hillsboro Village. If Nashville had a Greenwich Village, it would be Hillsboro Village. Fido is filled with mostly unrecognizable rock stars juxtaposed against wannabe rock stars who are noticeably trying too hard. There's a post-punk, authentic-looking guy sitting about three feet from me who is speaking with an Australian accent, and I swear to you—he has a rat-tail. The '80s are back in full effect, apparently. They've been coming back for the past few years, but the resurgence has peaked before my very eyes.

I vaguely remember the '80s, when my older sisters wore jean jackets covered in buttons over their Izod shirts with the collars flipped up, acid-washed jeans, bangs teetering on top of their heads. Similar to today, anything over-the-top was cool. Back then it was anything Madonna. Anything Boy George. My brothers, on the other hand, were listening to arena rock bands like Cinderella and Dokken. We weren't *allowed* to listen to any of it—crikey, we weren't even allowed to listen to Amy Grant's *Lead Me On* album (drums, electric guitars, other "demonic" instruments, etc.)—but all of my siblings hid their stash of music with the same fortitude as prisoners squirreling away their cigarettes. I distinctly remember when my dad discovered my brother's Judas Priest tape and smashed it with a hammer on our living room carpet.

Somewhere in the midst of all that '80s madness, John Cougar Mellencamp ("JCM," if you will) started creeping into my artistic subconscious. He was everyman, in his white T-shirt and classic blue jeans. Admittedly, he did go through a phase that might be considered "big hair," if you're defining it loosely. But ultimately, he was the blue-collar rocker, like some guy who works the weekly forty at the steel mill but still manages to make an album in his spare time. Very Kevin Bacon circa *Footloose*. JCM went against the grain of everything that mainstream music was endorsing at the time. He stood up for the small towns, the farmers, the most basic things in life. He was just so *un*-rock star. And that's what I loved about him.

Ditto Springsteen.

They shaped me—musically and socially—by their contributions. I think those are some of the reasons behind my desire to maintain smallness and some vestige of reality in this unbalanced profession. I remember a conversation with a well-meaning friend who said, "You know, your career would really skyrocket if you'd just hire a strategist. You could really go places." I told him, "I'm not really interested in skyrocketing. I like the ground."

I'm sure it's not easy to understand how an entertainer might not want to be hugely popular. I've only had a tiny spoonful of what some would call "fame," and I didn't like the taste it left in my mouth. I like it here, with the beautiful few who have joined me, and it's almost insulting to suggest that I should need or want something more, something like superstardom. It implies that where I am isn't good enough and that it couldn't possibly be anything more than an unsatisfying pit stop on the path to my *real* dreams.

* * *

There is a question that I am asked frequently that always frustrates me, because I feel like the question misses the point. It presents itself in several different manners, from "Are you famous?" to "Do you have a tour bus?" Despite the fact that I pull up *alone*, in a *Camry*, I get asked that question at nearly every show. I can't help but laugh at the mental image of me rolling into Simpsonville, South Carolina, at the helm of a big, empty tour bus, to play a show at a coffee shop. In addition to being financially unattainable, that would be a ridiculous waste of space, gas, and whatever things I demolished along my path.

Last week at one of my shows, I recognized a girl who had been at a show a few years back. I went over to say hello, and the first thing she asked was, "How famous are you now?" I wilted inside.

How am I supposed to answer that? "Well, I'm more famous than you are, but not as famous as Mick Jagger," or "I'm on the B-List for Diddy's Christmas party"?

I tried to explain to her that I work really hard not to measure my life by that kind of yardstick, but she wasn't interested in that answer. It seemed like she wanted me to give her the right to believe that she was in the presence of greatness. She was probably just trying to be nice, but sometimes the approach makes me a bit uneasy. When people need to know that I'm "important," I can't help but think that it only serves to validate their own sense of importance. And that makes me feel a little bit used.

I tend to lose my priorities when emphasis is placed on fame and fortune. I am entirely capable of becoming full of myself, and when I am constantly asked if I am famous or if I have a tour bus, I tend to focus on my pride and my net worth. I don't like the person I become when I focus on those things.

But a lot of people don't want to hear "the gospel of small-ness," about how I want to learn to focus less on myself and more on Jesus. They apparently want to think that five years from now they'll be able to show off the autographed photo to their friends or auction it off on eBay. So I usually just smile and keep my mouth shut, which is difficult for me. I see people's faces drop when I'm not able to be what they want me to be (i.e., rich and famous), and then I feel like a failure. Then I realize that I'm allowing people to dictate what success means to me. It's just a horrible cycle.

Honestly, it's weird to hear things like "When you're famous, I'll be able to tell all my friends, 'I knew her back in the day.'" What about *now?* Would they be talking to me if they knew that I would never be famous? It feels like I'm being promised their undying love and affection—so long as I live up to their expectations for me. But if I don't, then I'm a waste of time? The only lasting thing I have to offer people anyway is rooted in the unchanging fact that Jesus has redeemed me, not the fact that I play the guitar and write songs.

These questions seem to stem from the notion that fame is more desirable than lack of fame. I only have a few friends who would be considered "famous," but people always want me to list them off. "So you live in Nashville," they say. "Do you know any famous people? Like, rock stars and stuff? Do you know the girl who won *Nashville Star?*" The sad thing is that most of the "famous" people I do know are far more miserable than the average people I know. Based on the percentages, I'd take lack of fame any day.

A few years ago, I went out with a professional wrestler who was extremely well known in the world of wrestling fans. We were at Chicago O'Hare International Airport once, and I watched him do everything possible to avoid being noticed—to hold on to the little pieces of his life that he could still claim. Then, inevitably, someone who had been watching him for a while would finally muster the nerve to approach him.

The adrenaline of being recognized lasted for only a moment, leaving behind a paranoia about every action done thoughtlessly, every word that might've been overheard by someone who hadn't spoken up to ask for his autograph yet ... *Did I say anything personal before he approached me? Did I impatiently cut in line in front of her at the security checkpoint? Will this kid go home and tell all of his friends that his hero turned out to be a jerk?* He did not own his life, and that has a way of making a person feel powerless, regardless of how much power fame seems to afford him.

* * *

Jesus was a servant to those around Him, and He wasn't treated very well most of the time. We should expect the same thing if we want to be like Him. People don't roll out the red carpet for servants. Likewise, I should never expect to have a big Prevost tour bus. If God chooses to bless me with that at some point, that's great, but I think that's about as likely as winning the lottery.

I have to remind myself that God did not call me to be a rock star—He called me to express my salvation through music. And there is a vast difference. He made it very clear to me from the start that if I intended to follow Him, I should never expect more than having to drive eight hours to play for ten people who don't know who I am and don't care. They might not buy my CDs, and I might have to sleep in my car that night, before I get up and do it all over again the next day. I've done it—*many* times.

It was obvious from the beginning that, as much as I wanted it to be, this music thing was *not* going to be about me. So I'm trying hard to remember that. I fail miserably at it most of the time. I don't know how to step outside of myself enough yet. I end up getting proud of the fact that I am humble enough not to pursue fame.

It's like there's no way out of the problem—I don't know how to solve *me*. And it's something I struggle with every single day.

* * *

One morning not too long ago, I was trying to focus more on getting it right. I woke up and prayed a short prayer, asking God to help me live with humility that day. I remember it clearly because of what happened afterward.

I drove nine hours alone to get to the venue, and when I arrived, most of the crew treated me with total disregard. My sound check was two hours late, there was trouble with the merchandise table, and I had to shovel down my dinner right before the event started. Then the promoter told me that they'd be showing *Monday Night Football* on a Jumbotron behind me while I played the show.

I tried to make a joke about the Jumbotron: "Well, then, I'll try not to play any meaningful songs, like ... anything about *Jesus*."

But he replied, "It doesn't really matter, because nobody's going to be listening to you anyway."

By all accounts, I had never been treated so poorly by any venue anywhere.

There was someone scheduled to speak before I sang. Nasty thoughts started doing laps in my brain. *Wow, this guy is getting the royal treatment. Interesting how they don't make* him *speak in front of* Monday Night Football, *and I wonder how long* he *had to wait for a sound check.*

When he began to speak, he said his topic was servanthood. He referenced the story of Jesus washing the disciples' feet and said, "The higher you rise, the further you get from the feet." Sometimes, when I start to think I'm really cool, God allows me to trip and fall flat on my face so that I'm eye-level with those feet that need washing. It's humbling. I had to look back at that whole day and say, "Thank You, God, for answering my prayer and for reminding me that it's not about me. I keep forgetting."

This subject speaks as much about the sin inside of me as anyone else. I'm the one who has the harder time forgetting myself. All this "rich and famous" talk feeds the beast and puts the focus on the wrong priorities. The last thing musicians need is another reason to think about ourselves and our status more often.

While I've been sitting here at Fido, I've noticed my tendency to evaluate my status versus the status of every other musician in the room. *What shows has he played? How many albums has she sold? Do they have more fans?* I'll feel empowered the moment someone who merely does music part time walks in. If he has a "real" job, I can give myself one point against him. But the moment that my friend Matt walks in—he plays to sold-out crowds and makes more money in a month than I make in a year—all of the points I've accumulated will be wiped from the slate. As he tells me about his latest opportunities to showcase his music in films and on television, I make a mental note to stab myself in the eye and give my guitars to charity.

Up and down, up and down. My ego will inflate and deflate a dozen times if I sit here long enough, watching musicians come and go in this coffee shop. Mentally, that is such an unstable place to be. That instability is just another reason why I don't want to find my value there—not just because it's the wrong thing to do, but because it's so bipolar. I guess if it were a more permanent place, I might be more tempted to invest some self-esteem in it. But I'm glad that's not the case, because I might start to believe it. I don't want to find my worth in those things, even though I use that as my barometer *all the time*. Frankly, it's exhausting.

16

Highway to the Danger Zone

LAST WEEK I WAS DRIVING across Texas—from a Thursday-night show in Lubbock to a Friday-night show in Houston. I used three different mapping websites, and they gave me estimates ranging from eight hours and forty-nine minutes to twelve hours and fifty-three minutes. That seemed ridiculously long. So I made up my own route, crossing the state diagonally on two-lane highways. This would've been a good idea except for all of the small-town police officers hiding on the other side of every Dairy Queen, daring an out-of-state plate to cross their path.

I knew that I couldn't speed—no matter how long the drive—because of the two Texas speeding tickets I'd already accumulated this year. After the third hour, the drive began to wear on me. My back was aching, my eyes were growing heavy, plus there was the unbearable pain of abiding by the speed limit.

In west Texas, the sky swallows you. The earth is beautifully selfless; it demands no attention—it is flat and barren except for the occasional oil rig that probes into the ground. And even in the middle of November, the sun baked my car's interior. The heat and the unchanging scenery hypnotized me. By the time I got to Waco—about halfway through the drive—I was in desperate need of a cup of coffee. Despite the fact that I had stopped drinking coffee the year before due to an addiction that could mildly be described as "life-threatening," I rationalized that it was much more life-threatening to fall asleep at the wheel. So I pulled over to a familiar little coffee shop just off Interstate 35.

As I handed over my cash, it occurred to me that this was the first time I'd ever had to pay for coffee there. Before that day, I'd just summon the guy behind the counter: "Danger, can I get a cup of black?" He'd smile and hand me a cup, shaking his head at the money I tried to give him.

* * *

I met Danger a couple of summers ago when I played a concert at a Christian sports camp in Missouri. This particular camp was the former stomping ground of my manager at the time, so he and I went a few days early to hang out, meet people, and let him visit with old friends. Danger worked at the camp, leading outdoor adventure groups and doing some general upkeep on the camp-grounds.

For three meals a day, my manager and I ate in the cafeteria at large picnic tables with all of the staff and campers. On our second morning there, I grabbed a bowl of Cheerios and went to our usual table by the window. The only empty spot was between my manager and a striking, tan guy with a black bandana covering his dark hair. When I sat down, he turned to me and said, "Who are you, and why are you here?" I normally would've been taken aback by his abruptness, but it came in a warm tone. Plus, he was devastatingly handsome.

"I'm here hanging out with my friend for a few days," I said as my knees buckled.

I am somewhat reluctant to tell people that I'm a musician because it usually alters their view of me and changes the course of the conversation dramatically. So I skirted the real answer and tried to find out who *he* was.

He was from New Jersey but was about to start his senior year at a college in Waco, where we discovered we actually had a few friends in common. I had played concerts at his college too, but I didn't bring that up. I teased him about his love for New Jersey and his disdain for Texas, because I love Texas as though it were my own, and I told him so. "If they ever invent a plastic surgery to change a person's state of origin, I'm going to have it, and I'm going to be from Texas."

He made a face like he'd just seen a three-car pileup. I gently reminded him of the perils of messing with Texas, and he offered a sinister laugh in return. We were off to a grand start.

I nicknamed him "Danger" when he started talking about his affinity for wild adventures and extreme sports. He came across as an outdoorsy kind of guy, like the kind of guy who would probably have a hemp necklace and a hookah. And I noticed that he said "right on" a lot.

He was eating pancakes.

"What, no granola?" I asked him.

"Are you calling me a *hippie*?" he said, faking offense.

"If the Birkenstock fits," I responded.

He pointed to his feet to show that he was actually wearing an old pair of black Converse. I wasn't sure how to peg him. Not a hippie, not a hipster, but something in between. We talked about music; he listened to a lot of bands that I didn't know much about. From their names, I gathered that they were indie/punk bands. I think the only band we both liked was Weezer or maybe Guster. We talked all through breakfast, and I don't remember speaking to anyone else at the table. It took us a long time to finish our food. My Cheerios got soggy. I didn't care.

That afternoon, I saw him painting some buildings at camp, and I talked to him a little more. He mentioned something about liking the trees there, so I gave him one of my stickers that says "Trees Are Cool," which is based on a song that I wrote by the same name. He looked at me in shock.

"Are *you* the girl who plays on campus sometimes?" he asked.

"Yes ... that would be me," I said reluctantly.

I was a little bit sad to let the mystery go because I was afraid he'd start thinking of me differently. Sometimes people might like me less if they think my music is bad, or they might like me more if they think that being a musician is cool. I'd rather have people base their opinions of me on something other than my career.

* * *

That night I played a concert for the campers, and he hung around after the crowd disappeared. We talked for a long time again, and I remember being very aware of the fact that I looked like poo. My hair was frizzy from the relentless humidity, and I was really sweaty from playing the show. The right side of my abdomen always gets soaked with sweat from where my guitar rests against it. So I had this big sweaty spot on the right side of my body, and there he stood, talking to me for probably two whole hours.

He got my CD, and when he put it in his bag, I noticed that he had a lot of books inside. That intrigued me. I'm a sucker for smart guys who read a lot. I caught the title of one of the books: *The Sickness Unto Death.*

"So ... Kierkegaard, eh?" I asked.

"Yeah, I'm a philosophy major. I mean, this isn't assigned reading for the summer or anything, but I just think it's fascinating," he said.

Jackpot.

He offered to help me carry my guitars to my car, and we walked very slowly. Somehow, he made me do everything in slow motion. We stood by my car after we put the guitar cases inside. Mosquitoes assaulted me. I was still sweaty. None of that mattered. I wrote my initials in the gravel with the toe of my shoe during the somewhat-awkward moment where we exchanged phone numbers and emails. And then I didn't really sleep that night.

We ate breakfast together again the next morning. He was quiet and reserved, but what he did say carried so much intensity. Over French toast and orange juice, he told me that he had lived and worked in a Bolivian orphanage the previous summer and that his life's ambition was to move back to South America and start a revolution that would change the way things happened there. He said the people there were so real—passionate and unencumbered by greed. He said he loved them.

I have never been to South America, and I have no desire to give up all my worldly goods to move to Bolivia. So Danger and I were definitely on different tracks, but his track was intriguing and seemed holier than mine. Playing music for a living involves quite a bit of self-glorification, especially when compared to being a missionary at an orphanage. His passion for Jesus and his love for people made him the most vibrant person in the room. I was sad that there had been moments when he had been breathing near me that I had missed because I wasn't paying attention.

* * *

That morning after breakfast, I had to make the eight-hour drive back to Nashville. I hoped he would say something of significance before I left, something indicating an interest in me, so that I wouldn't have to wonder if it was just me. Even an "I really like talking to you; I'm excited to get to know you better" would've been nice. But I got nothing.

A few weeks after I left, he emailed me, and we began exchanging lengthy emails and three-hour phone calls.

"How long have you been interested in South America?" I asked him one night on the phone. I blew into my green tea to cool it off a little before drinking it.

"Since I became a Communist," he said.

"When was ... wait ... *what?* You're a *Communist?*" I asked. I spilled tea down the front of my shirt.

"You betcha," he said. I could hear the smile in his voice.

"So, we're pretty much the exact opposite of each other," I said, laughing at the irony.

"Pretty much. Except that we both love Jesus," he said.

"And sushi!" I offered.

"Well, yes. There's that," he laughed.

* * *

I played at his college again that September, so we spent a few days together. It was still very hard to figure out his interest level. His actions said he was interested, but he never spoke of it. I felt like a fool for not knowing. A few months later, he told me that he had been in a relationship when we met and that he had been in the early stages of ending things. That helped explain things a little bit, but it also added to the general confusion.

One night after he told me that, we were hanging out at his house, and it started to rain. He had a tin-roofed garage, so he grabbed coats for us and we ran out to stand under the roof so we could hear the rain. It was three in the morning and he had class at eight, but he stayed up to talk to me. He said it would be a waste of his time *not* to talk to me because there was nothing he'd rather do than have good conversation. Not even sleep. Statements like that help me understand a little bit of the way that God feels about me. I reveled in it.

We stood there with our Syrah and talked in the dark as the rain pounded the sheets of tin above our heads. This seemed like a pretty romantic thing to do, and that was when it started to become clearer in his words and actions that he was interested in me. I didn't dare ask him to lay it out, but I wanted to. I didn't want to be his girlfriend, per se. I didn't want him to "define the relationship"—I just wanted him to define the *direction.*

We went upstairs after nearly an hour outside, and I fell asleep on his couch. The next day I packed up to leave, taking my unanswered questions with me.

> *But tension is to be loved*
> *When it is like a passing note*
> *To a beautiful, beautiful chord.*
> **—SIXPENCE NONE THE RICHER,**
> "Tension Is a Passing Note"

* * *

Those scenes with Danger flashed through my head while I was waiting on my to-go coffee in that Waco coffee shop. I didn't have time to stick around there, at that ghost-town coffee shop where he used to work, because I had to get back on the road to Houston. It wasn't the same without him there, anyway. The room felt empty, less alive. I wanted that familiarity; it was one of the reasons why I had stopped—to have one of those brief, all-too-uncommon moments where I can connect with someone who knows who I am, someone who can bring me a handful of community when I'm starving for it on the road.

I think my memories did more to wake me up than the coffee did. I left feeling alert and alone.

17

Yardsticks

American Airlines Flight 1406: October 2005

ONE OF THE CONSISTENT THEMES in my life is that I tend to fall for guys who want to move to third-world countries and become missionaries. The desire to do that is not at all in my makeup, so I have to wonder if I'm picking the wrong guys, if I'm supposed to be a missionary and just don't realize it, or if maybe I am not supposed to be married.

In addition to that, I've never been one to dream of having children—the jury is still out on that. Most of the guys I meet are already talking about what they will name their sons or daughters, whereas I just think about whether or not we'd have a deer mounted above our fireplace. I have a heart condition that pretty much prevents me from having kids anyway, so maybe that is God's way of setting things in stone. Adoption is always an alternative, but like I said, I'm not even sure I want kids, and adoption is not exactly something you should do halfheartedly.

A woman at church told me that she thinks that people who can't have kids (or don't want them) are not supposed to be married, because God gave the command to "be fruitful and multiply." Her opinion triggers two thoughts: First, God gave that command *to Adam and Eve*, not the population at large. So if we're going to start up with the business of applying His specific commands to the entire universe, then we should all trot our son Isaac up to the mountain and sacrifice him. Second, it makes me wonder what she thinks of couples who lose children to miscarriage or who find out after they are married that they have reproductive difficulties—were they just completely "outside of God's plan" for getting married in the first place? You can't know those things in advance.

I told Kemper what this woman said to me—about how I was supposed to never get married—and he said, in words that I will censor here for your benefit, that her statement was the biggest load of crap he had ever heard. That, of course, reassured me that I still have a chance of not being single for the rest of my life.

Singleness is fun, actually. It would be a lie to act like I didn't enjoy it. I get to fly around the country and visit enchanting places and be more selfish than I should be, without having it personally affect many people other than myself. Sometimes I think about how none of this would've happened—this dream, this life, this *me*—had it not been for Antonio moving in and out of my life. Part of me wants to thank him. Sometimes I imagine what it would be like to run into him somewhere when I'm on tour—at baggage claim in an airport, on a street corner, on the subway. But I finally know that I'm okay with never seeing him again.

*   *   *

Right now, I am on a plane that just left Dallas for Newark, and I'm looking down at the rows of Texas housing developments—I call them House Farms, because it's like they're growing rows of brand-new houses, complete with the token maple in the front yard, intended to somehow replace the entire forest that they cut down in order to accommodate said House Farm. From miles above, I'm casting shadows on other people's lawns in the suburban pseudo-jungle. I'm looking down at these houses, wondering if I will ever live there with Someone Yet to Be Named.

And I think of Harry. We haven't spoken since he sent the "I'm Ceasing All Contact" email, other than a short phone conversation in which he asked me to tell him that I hate him—to just say it out loud—so I did. It felt like stolen treasure, glorious and guilty all at once.

*   *   *

He still shows up in my brain at frustratingly unexpected times. For instance, he used to tell me that crossing my legs would jack up my spine and make my back hurt, and he was right. So I started making a conscious effort to stop doing it. And now, every time that I mindlessly cross—and then actively uncross—my legs, I have to spend the subsequent twenty minutes trying to assassinate his memory. It's like my mind is a giant suitcase with a broken latch, and I have to keep a death grip on it with both hands at all times—otherwise, all these things will spill out on the ground, and it will take me forever to clean them up again.

So you lingered, I took you with me
Through the country, every city—
Thinking I'd be better off that way.
—MATT WERTZ, "Over You"

I daydream of Someone who is like him but who is in love with me. Hot Nathan is my backup, in case Someone never finds me. Hot Nathan and I have known each other for five years, and all my friends started calling him Hot Nathan because we knew three Nathans and, well, he was the hot one. Hot Nathan and I kissed one humid summer night a long time ago, and he is the only boy I've ever kissed that I still speak to. He's the only twenty-three-year-old single guy I know who wants to marry every girl he meets. Hot Nathan and I decided that if we're both single by the time I'm thirty-five, then we will get married.

On the other hand, my brother Jason wants me to marry Andy Beard, a funny blond guy from North Carolina whom I met at church camp when I was seventeen. We had a brief long-distance relationship in high school, and he came to visit me a few times and meet my family. Jason liked Andy because Andy reminded him of a younger version of himself. They are both sweet and funny, and they both love dirt bikes. When Andy took me to my debutante ball—which had a very strict policy for attire—he secretly wore a blinking bow tie. That thoroughly cemented Jason's desire to have him in the family.

To this day, I can't bring a guy home without Jason surreptitiously mouthing "Andy Beard" across the dinner table. I haven't seen Andy since my senior year of high school, and he may even be married by now, but Jason still insists that I hold out for him, wherever he is, just in case.

But Harry is the closest thing I have to a yardstick. No matter how much we fought and disagreed, I knew that I would've been willing to stick it out forever and keep trying, because of how much I loved him and how much he made me want to be better. I have had to train myself not to be loyal to him any longer, because while I couldn't imagine that there was anything else I could want in Someone, I was not enough for him.

The pilot is interrupting my train of thought (thankfully) by telling us that Delaware is the only state without a commercial airport. Apparently we are over Delaware now. I know that we will be passing New York City soon, just before we land in Newark. I always try to get a seat on the right side of the plane when flying into the City, and on the left side when flying out, because I know that means I will have a view of that twenty-three-square-mile island that I love so much. And I wonder again when God will make it clear to me whether or not He wants me to move there. It is not a city you should move to by accident, so I need Him to be insistent with me.

18

Setting the Record Straight

Seattle, Washington: August 2005

I AM SITTING IN THE ABANDONED bedroom of a girl I have never met. I am occupying her former room for the night, because this is the home of the people who were kind enough to put me up for this particular evening of the tour. I look around the room to see walls covered with photographs of the girl with all of her friends. There was a day when my life and friendships could be captured in a photo collage on my wall. Those days are over. My walls are changing every day.

These days, my friends are scattered across the globe in all the places I've traveled. Some of them are people I've met at shows, which means that I don't get to see them unless I'm touring in their area and they come to the show. Some of them are musicians who, like me, travel constantly. Seeing them is even rarer. We have to browse each other's websites, check tour dates and compare them with our own, then call and see if there's maybe half an hour after sound check when we can grab a cup of coffee and talk about our bizarre lives. This is the sad summary of my social life. Being gone nearly three hundred days a year doesn't afford me any other option.

I still miss Harry a lot sometimes. He had so many of the qualities that I want in Someone—namely, a white-collar brain and blue-collar hobbies. He loved Jesus. He was a well-read businessman who hunted deer and played football. He had thighs the size of tree trunks (which is my secret weakness). And he held all the doors and deferred to me first whenever we were ordering food at a restaurant. His attention to detail was unparalleled, and he knew how to read through female-speak as though it were his native language. He did not want to be a missionary. And I never grew tired of being near him.

He was the only consistent thing in my life for a long time. Every day, he would call to check up on me, find out how my day was, and say something to hurt my feelings, followed by something that gave me the irrational hope that someday he would stop dating girls he barely knew and finally realize he loved the girl he knew like the back of his hand. *How can I still be this broken?*

Last night, as I was packing for my flight, I ran across one of my favorite books of poetry from high school, and I found where I had earmarked W.H. Auden's "Stop All the Clocks." I cried and remembered back when Harry and I used to talk for hours, sometimes just sitting on the phone while we worked, for no other reason than to hear each other breathe and make the occasional comment.

I miss having someone in my day-to-day.

I am able in all of my travels
To make these memories quit.
But tonight, I clearly recall
Every little bit.
—PATTY GRIFFIN, "Every Little Bit"

* * *

Chicago, Illinois: October 2005

Just a few nights ago, I seized some time with a friend who is a fairly well-known musician. We sat in the empty auditorium, talking about the struggle he is experiencing at this point in his career. Long after the crowds had gone home, he and I sat there in the dark as he posed questions without answers. We talked for nearly an hour about how there seems to be no right direction.

God has grown his career—which he knows is a huge blessing—but now he feels stranded at the top of the ladder. He kicked his feet up on the back of the chair in front of him and ran his hands through his hair, grabbing fistfuls. Then he told me that when success started to come upon him, he couldn't help but feel burdened by the size of it. I imagine that when that kind of thing happens, all you would want is to plant your feet firmly on the ground. But on the other hand, the thought of descent would be terrifying.

This is a lonely place. I don't say that to elicit pity. I just need to say it to make it real, to defeat the myth that living your dream will solve everything. Fame and fortune don't solve it (not that I have either), and from what I've witnessed, they actually seem to make it worse. My famous friend feels even more of a burden than I do.

Humans need stability somewhere—something that can't leave or be taken away. A place to call home. I have that, but not without exception. Home always brings the reminder that I have been gone for too long. The last time I went home, my six-year-old niece couldn't remember my name. Later that same day, my seven-year-old niece asked me what my job was. I tried to help her figure it out on her own, so I asked, "Well, think about it for a minute—what one thing do I do a lot of?" And her answer broke my heart: "Mostly, you just go away."

*   *   *

I'm starting to wonder if the reason this doesn't feel like home is because it *isn't*. I keep thinking that if I can just live in the right place, furnished (nicely, but not too ostentatiously) with Restoration Hardware furniture and Pottery Barn lamps, and if I can hang out with the cool kids and attend the hip church, then everything will work together to fill the gaping hole inside of me. It's a pretty little pipe dream.

But no matter the size of my crowds or how impressed my friends are when they walk into my house, I still feel the longing for Home. I love my job—it is my dream come true—but I still ache for something that will last. I long for Eden, and this will never be it. We were built for more, and even audiences full of fans who hang on to your every word can't make that longing go away.

19

Me, Myself, & I

WHEN YOU SPEND AS MUCH TIME ALONE as I do, it's
pretty easy to get settled into yourself. And since I usually tour
alone, I get to choose the songs on the radio, the cuisine for each
meal, the time I go to bed, and the specific truck-stop chain to
frequent. It's hard to remember that the world is not, in fact, pulled
toward my gravity. In an effort to remind myself of this, I've been
trying to take mental notes whenever someone strikes me as par-
ticularly selfless, and I've been spending more time in my community, feeling out the needs of my friends and watching the way they
serve people. It reminds me of what I want to be like.

I'm also a bit of a documentary freak, and a lot of the things
I've watched lately have been so challenging to me. I just watched
a documentary on the Masai tribe of Africa. They live on the
border of Kenya and Tanzania. They build houses out of sticks
and cow dung, paint their faces with the blood of animals they've

killed, and dance animatedly around their campfires.

Just a little reminder: I live in a two-story stone house with a constant temperature of seventy-two degrees, I wear uncomfortable stilettos just because I think they're pretty, and I pay upward of $10 to see a movie. Now, back to my point ...

Several months after the tragedies of 9/11, word of the events traveled across the ocean, through the wilderness, and to the edge of a Masai campfire. The people described the events to each other in detail, with hand motions depicting the airplanes crashing into the high-rise buildings. Most of the Masai people have probably never even seen a skyscraper. But they sat around their campfire with tears in their eyes. And these warriors were so brokenhearted by what they heard that they were moved to donate their most valuable possession—their cattle, their source of food and means of labor—to the people of New York City.

The Masai and their cattle ... The widow and her coins ... And me, calculating the exact number of my feeble 10 percent tithe, if even that.

*   *   *

In another documentary that I watched recently, the filmmakers interviewed the children of Afghanistan, asking them what they want to be when they grow up. These kids, who have never known anything but poverty and war, said things like "I want to be a doctor so I can help people" or "I just want to go to college." Not a single one of them said they wanted to be a movie star or a rock star. It's so unlike the culture I have known.

There was an interview with a thirteen-year-old boy who teaches English to younger kids every day. I can't even imagine it. These kids live in an atmosphere of anger and hatred, but they seem to have a persistent hope that cannot be quenched. No one has told them that college is virtually impossible. All they hope for is something more than hopelessness.

I wish I were the kind of person who gave up everything to help those kids attain the life they dream of having. Maybe someday I will be. My friend Beth is like that. She started a nonprofit to help the underprivileged kids in one of Houston's poorest neighborhoods. Tonight it was unseasonably cold in Houston, and Beth gave her coat to a sixth-grade girl who didn't have one. The girl asked her for it, and Beth took it off and gave it to her. Just like that. There was no "I have one at home that I'll bring you tomorrow," while mentally fishing through her closet to think of her least desirable coat. She just handed it over.

Things like that make me so aware of how deeply set I am in my own ways. I was confessing to Jane recently, telling her about my ever-present struggle to "die to self"—there's so much that I'm clinging to. I told her, "This whole 'becoming a better person' thing ... I hate it."

How has He not given up on me yet? How can I see what I'm supposed to be so clearly, and yet every day go back to being who I've always been?

Did You come to make me new
And know I'd crawl right back into the skin You found me in?
—NICHOLE NORDEMAN, "Live"

Maybe that's why it's so amazing to see Him actually change my heart in an unexpected way. He surprises me with it sometimes, and I am stopped in my tracks, happy to meet Him there. I see it happen in other people, too—this noticeable change taking place, like it did with my dad—and I love the little reminders that this is real, that His persistent love is actually what makes the changes happen. And I'm *even* more amazed by the fact that He loves me *before* I get to that place of change.

* * *

One of the girls at Tuesday Night Jesus Club always has the most annoying prayer requests. We go around the room at the end of the Bible study, and everybody says things like "I'm really mad at my boss right now, and I need prayer to be able to tolerate him another day," or "I'm not sure I'm going to have enough money to go on the group vacation this year, and I really want to ... could you pray that God will provide for that?"

But every single time, Katie asks for us to pray for something like "patience" or "faith" or "humility," and I want to roll my eyes at her. She says things like "The past few days have been really tough and stressful at home, so I just want to ask you to pray that God will help me be humble enough to understand that my life isn't supposed to be a bed of roses." It's like she's trying to put on a show of how perfect she is, except it's real. I can't believe it.

I've seen other people who come across as humble, but mostly I think that humility is just getting confused with shyness. They aren't selfless, they're just quiet. I remember being backstage at a show in Abilene, Texas, one time, and I heard a girl describe another musician by saying, "He *radiates* humility." She said it all dreamy, like it made her weak in the knees. And I remember thinking, *What's the big deal? I can do that—I can make you believe I'm humble*, because it can be so contrived sometimes. Maybe I'm just messing with semantics, but the very nature of humility seems to be that it doesn't really radiate at all—it doesn't draw attention to itself.

Katie is like that. I am not. Neither of us are quiet people; we both talk a lot, actually. But something in her words makes it evident that she's not trying to win merit badges for humility.

One of the few other times I've seen someone be that authentically humble—or what seems to be authentic, as far as I can tell—was last year, when I was touring with my friend Josh. The first day or two, I spent a lot of time writing songs about Harry, since I was still reeling from those wounds. I worked on my *Love Is a Choice* workbook and tried to learn how to step outside of myself a little more. It was hard to be in a cordial mood, but no matter what my temperament, Josh treated me with nothing less than complete kindness.

We talked a lot during the drives, about music and writing and guys and girls. He helped me see the truth about some of the things I was dealing with in regard to Harry and encouraged me to delete the expletives from my songs about him and to start caring about other people again.

I imagine this is what Jesus would be like, intercepting the anger and replacing it with love. Josh managed to show me tenderness even when I was at my worst. In a lot of ways, I think that's the ultimate display of humility—when someone lays down his rights and preferences in order to show deference to someone else.

There was zero "radiation"—just an obvious kindness that contradicted all of my emotions. That kind of thing changes me quicker than anything.

* * *

When I'm around people who are more humble than I am, it's an odd thing—it creates a sort of ambivalence within me. Part of me is challenged to be more like them, and part of me is frustrated by them. The problem with Danger is that I have always felt like he is a far better person than I am. More sanctified. He cares about better things than I do, better things than most people. Dating him is probably like dating Mother Teresa.

When he and I were getting to know each other more intentionally, he came up from Texas for a visit. We drove up to the mountains one night, and he found a grassy area with giant oak trees by a private lake. It was starting to get pretty cold, so I dug through my luggage and piled on a few extra layers of clothes while he went to find a place for us to sit.

When I made it over to the lake, I found that he had put out a green cotton blanket and some paper cups from a gas station. He set up my laptop on the blanket, and we sat there and watched a movie and drank from the paper cups. The laptop died halfway through the movie, but it was a clear night, so we stayed there for a while and talked. I shivered. My socks had gotten wet from walking through the grass, and my feet were starting to freeze. I tucked them up under his legs, but it didn't help much.

That was when I started unpacking my thoughts about "us."

"The problem with us," I told him, "is that if we spent a concentrated amount of time together, we wouldn't fit. We would start to hate each other. We work well in these short-term encounters, but if we really had to dig into chunks of time, we would be too different."

"What do you mean?" he asked. "How could it be that bad?"

"Well, you would start to say things to me like 'Tara Leigh, what makes you think it's okay to spend $40 on a pair of shoes?' And I would say things to you like 'Danger, do we really have to take the homeless guy to dinner with us again tonight?'"

He tried to point out that he didn't think $40 was a lot to spend on new shoes, but then I reminded him that he'd been wearing the same pair of Chucks for eight years. I also had my doubts that someone as sacrificial as he was could legitimately care about someone as selfish as me once he got to know me well enough to see past my attempts to hide my sins. But I didn't tell him that part.

For at least another hour, we lay there talking, shaking from the cold, looking up through the trees, cementing the moment into our history. I don't know why we stayed there instead of getting in the car and cranking up the heat, except that it was a beautiful moment.

"Danger"
—TARA LEIGH COBBLE

First glimpses over pancakes and cereal bowls
And waking up to knowing you—
The tan skin of long days spent coloring the summer sky
Peeking from beneath the blue shirt, the blue paint.

You strange case, with your shy grin, your boyish laugh ...
And all the while, hiding Kierkegaard in your backpack!

Your shoes gave you away, that we are not the same—
"Not at all the same," we would learn to say.
And those differences wrapped around us like a hurricane
Holding us still and untouched in its eye ...

Like the autumn night you held me on the mountain
We stood, paused, in the air of the coming morning—
The lingering moment, still not moment enough ...
When you drew me out, drew me in, drew me close.

Your guard, your discretion, your resolve—
They are stronger than nearly anything ... except your words.

HERE'S TO HINDSIGHT

Your words: The earth moved and shifted
To bring us into the room where you came to meet me ...
While knowing nothing of me, my life, my heart—
And even still, I barely know you ... but you asked me to try.

So we lay side by side on the grass, like the threads of the blanket,
We stood under the tin roof, under the cold rain—
And as if the hurricane weren't relentless enough ...
Here we are again, stranger. Here we are ... for now.

What now?

20

In Circles

A FEW MONTHS AFTER THAT NIGHT in the mountains with Danger, I was on tour in Texas, and I stopped to play at his college. He sat about five feet away from me, and I could barely stand to look at him because he was so beautiful. I managed to look over at Danger once during the third or fourth song. He smiled at me, but I could tell that he was sad. I kept playing, focusing mostly on playing the happier songs, but he kept looking sad. Near the end of my set, he got up and left.

I stopped by his house after the show and found him sitting at his computer, looking up flights to Bolivia.

"What happened to you?" I asked. He told me that he saw me come alive when I was onstage and that he wanted to come alive again too. He said he couldn't do that as long as he was in America, where selfish gain and commerce and power struggles are so prominent. He looked desperate. I tried to talk him out of it, tried to tell him that people are selfish and sinful everywhere, not just here. But he made some annoying point about how God had put this thing in him that made him only be able to think about how much he wanted to help the people that Jesus talked about helping, people like the orphans he had lived with in Bolivia. He said *they* are what make him come alive inside—they are *his* song on a stage.

It was early December and he only had a semester left in college, but he wanted to drop out and give away all of his things and move to Bolivia the next week. He said he was looking around his room, thinking of what he could give to whom. It made him so excited to think about giving away all this stuff—his stereo to his roommate, his computer to his brother, his clothes to Goodwill.

That sounded completely insane to me. I thought about my PowerBook and my iPod, and I felt wrong for wanting to keep them. I felt certain that God liked him more than me, even though that is contrary to God's nature. Danger was so weird and enthralling, and even though I admired him, I couldn't make myself be like him, as hard as I tried.

* * *

Danger decided to stay in school after all, mainly out of respect for the money his parents had spent on his tuition. Over the holidays, I went up to New York City to spend a week hanging out there, and I got to meet his family for the first time. Their New Jersey home is very tall with a cute yard, just a few feet from their neighbors on both sides. It's like someone grabbed their neighborhood on both ends and smashed it together so that everything got really tall and much closer together. *Condense-a-hood.*

His family is wealthy—cherry-wood sleigh beds and ornately framed original art—but he renounces that lifestyle. He doesn't buy new clothes or gadgets, and he reminds me of Rich Mullins with his strange, vagabond, vow-of-poverty ways. *This man would fit in well with my "three ice cubes" family,* I thought, *but the Communism thing probably wouldn't fly.*

Each morning, I spent half an hour getting ready while he read books and waited for me, and then we took the train into the City. I was in love with it. We brought books for the ride—mine was *Me Talk Pretty One Day*, a book of humorous modern essays by David Sedaris, and his was Jean-Paul Sartre's *Nausea*. We rode and read, and occasionally he looked over at me and smiled, then—without a word—went back to reading again. Our level of comfort made me feel so at home.

On the subways and in the streets, relentless panhandlers preyed on all the holiday-season tourists. I'd been to the City many times, but I'd never seen even half that much panhandling at one time. I was kind of annoyed.

One kid impressed me, though. He came onto the train and announced that he was selling candy for a dollar, just to help keep him out of trouble. I bought some peanut M&Ms and Danger got plain M&Ms, and I felt good about myself that I had helped someone I thought was legitimate. *I've been a good steward,* I told myself as I bit into a yellow M&M. For all I know, the kid might've used the money to fund his meth lab, but I respected his entrepreneurial efforts enough not to explore the possibilities.

Danger, on the other hand, gave money to everyone who asked. He said he gives what he can and just trusts God to do the rest, to make sure they don't spend it on drugs and booze. It seemed generous and foolish all at the same time. I'm still not sure I'm comfortable with giving money, but I feel like I can't go wrong by helping someone get something to eat. And even if all I can do is smile at someone, that's at least a small piece of kindness I can offer.

* * *

One time I ate dinner with a homeless man in Atlanta, and he told me that it helps him not to have to fight the temptation to buy drugs if people will either buy him food or give him gift certificates. So I went out that day and bought some McDonald's gift certificates. I try to keep some with me when I'm in the City, because this seems like the best way for me to make sure I don't mess up my efforts to help people.

Regardless of whether or not I agreed with Danger's actions, I admired his heart and his motives. When I first met him, I asked him to tell me about his friends. I found out later that a few of the people he listed were homeless people. As long as I've known him, he has worn a little red and yellow bracelet that one of his homeless friends gave him.

A few times when I was with him, that friend called him and told him that she was hungry, and he went down to KFC and bought a bucket of chicken and took it to her. He had such patience about it, too. On one of my better days I might've done it, but I would've done it begrudgingly. He did it like he wanted to. It reminded me of my parents and the way they take every opportunity to share the love of Jesus with every single person who crosses their paths. And I couldn't help but think that if Danger ever had a big brown van, he'd have to leave for church two hours early, too.

On the night before New Year's Eve, we went ice-skating at Wollman Rink in Central Park—the one in all the movies. But it was not at all like it is in the movies. There were so many people packed onto the ice, skating in sync, that it felt like we were all fixed in one place and the ice was doing the rotations. We skated and froze and barely spoke a word. He was a hockey player, so he skated like a champ whenever there was a break in the crowd. I watched him with silent admiration. I kept thinking how I wanted "us" to make sense. But it didn't.

> *I got a weakness for strong chemistry*
> *One touch—all my resolutions change.*
> *I can say this is no good for me*
> *But I'm back for more of the same.*
> —DAVID WILCOX, "Strong Chemistry"

They cleared the ice at ten o'clock so that a guy could propose to his girlfriend from the center of the rink. She said yes as she cried and nearly fell over. It was a sweet, awkward moment, because a love story was unfolding in front of us, and Danger and I both knew that we were headed nowhere.

* * *

Sometimes I manage to get an inch of my body to move outside of my selfish shell. I'll start to feel a strong sense of urgency, like God is calling my heart to action. Maybe it's prompted by the part of me that feels like I need to have some actions to *prove* my faith, but maybe it's just that I'm falling in love with Him and it's the natural outpouring of my heart. I hope that's what it is.

Last week I went to a Christian bookstore in Colorado Springs. I headed straight for the doctrinal books or the ones with titles like *How to Grow Closer*. Then I stood there, frustrated with myself, when I realized that I spend so much time trying to fix myself—but for what? When do I ever love the people who need it?

I think maybe God would rather have me spend an hour loving someone—feeding the guy on the corner, raking my elderly neighbor's leaves—than memorizing Pauline doctrine. And here I am at my computer in Fido, growing in hypocrisy with every passing sentence that I type. I know for a fact that there are three homeless guys smoking by the door out back right now. Still I sit, measuring myself against the fashion icon sitting beside me.

21

Underwater Epiphanies

THERE IS A PLACE in the book of 1 John where John says that we are compelled to love because of the love we have received.

When I toured in Hawaii last year, I had one main goal: to hike into Mauna Loa, an active volcano in the center of the Big Island. Before my friend Kelly and I left on the trip, people kept telling me about how beautiful the water there is. And that's all well and good, because I like staring at the ocean as much as the next person—but I've held an abiding fear of deep water for most of my life.

When I was a little girl, my family visited my cousins in Fort Lauderdale, Florida, every summer. My older cousin Scott tormented me endlessly. His favorite means of doing this was by holding me underwater in the deep end of their pool, with my face close to the drain or that big roaming device that cleans the pool (theirs was called "The Barracuda," which only added to my terror). I fought him off as best I could, kicking against the water and throwing fists in the general direction of his head, until he finally realized it was time to let me go because drowning your younger cousin is probably a deterrent to picking up chicks. Then I would surface, gasping.

Sometimes our families went water-skiing in the Florida canals, and Scott told me stories about the skiers who had been attacked by the resident alligators. When I was waiting in the water for the boat to pull me up, things beneath the dark, murky water would brush against my legs and I would panic: *Alligator?!* Although I am a fairly decent swimmer, I still have trouble going into deep water, especially when I can't see the bottom. Sometimes I can even freak myself out if I sit on the edge of the deep end of a swimming pool in broad daylight. It's kind of stupid.

* * *

As I sat on the beach in Hawaii, I rubbed the black lava sand off my feet and legs. The mountains rose behind me. Despite the fact that it was only February, brilliant shades of green and blue dominated the landscape. I watched people parasailing and surfing, their tanned bodies flying through the air and across the water. The whole island was replete with the feeling of freedom and abandon, and I guess it seeped into me a little bit. I decided that it was time to defeat my fear of deep water. Snorkeling seemed to be the least threatening option because you stay relatively close to the surface of the water. I asked Kelly if she was up for it. I sort of hoped she'd say no, but she didn't.

The next day, we paid our $80 and set sail on a catamaran into the Pacific. They gave us brief instructions about how not to die, but mostly we were left on our own. Kelly and I strapped on the flippers and various pieces of thoroughly attractive headgear and then jumped into the ocean, as I prayed that God would help me override my fear with this newfound determination. We were swimming beside a coral reef when I had an unexpected burst of stupidity and decided to swim past the edge of it. Suddenly, there were places where I could not see the bottom of the ocean. It was scary. And beautiful. And I loved it. It was almost like my fear enhanced my awe.

During the ninety minutes we were in the ocean, I saw parts of creation that were entirely new to me. Kelly surfaced at one point and yelled over to me, "Did you see that?! That eel just had a baby!" I'm not sure that is possible because I think eels lay eggs, but regardless of the science of it, I was in the middle of one of those moments where I felt small and insignificant in comparison to everything around me.

Then it occurred to me that, of all these amazing, beautiful things, *I* am the thing that is made in God's image. I am given the distinct privilege of being called His daughter. Even when my guitar is out of tune and my fashion is bad, even when I'm getting angry because everyone at my show is talking instead of listening. I felt so overwhelmed that I started crying, right there in the Pacific. I don't recommend that, because strange things happen when your mask fogs up and you're inhaling salt water through the plastic tube. But I learned more that day about how God's love for me is so strangely attractive.

How could You consider me
So much more than all I see?
'Cause I am not, have never been,
Beautiful like this.
—JOSH WILSON, "Beautiful Like This"

It made Him more irresistible to me. When I feel His pull, hear His call, there is a stronger desire to follow. His love for me makes me love Him back. I just keep trying to think of ways to show Him that I love Him, and it is hard sometimes because He's not available in easily tangible ways—I can't hug Him or cook dinner for Him or look at Him with awe in my eyes.

Except that I realized ... He is.

Jesus said that we should treat other people the way we would treat Him. He said that if we do something nice for someone else, we are doing something nice for Him. He has identified Himself with all of us. He is the corporate CEO, the trust-fund socialite, the guy who sits alone at church every single Sunday, three rows from the back. He is my mailman, my roommate, and the guy named Ron who lives in an alley off Twelfth Avenue and asks me to bring him Mountain Dew. And I'm sure we've heard all this before, but it's still just as convicting to me when I let myself think about it.

I want to learn to love these people more than I love myself because somehow, that is loving God back. I'm still pretty horrible at it, and that's something I've learned firsthand from touring with other people. I never knew how bad I was until God dropped me down in that situation where I had to coexist with other people for long periods of time.

* * *

For a while now, I've been practicing this new mental exercise, mostly while I'm in traffic or on the subway: I scan the faces, look at their eyes, and tell myself, *She's precious to Jesus. He's precious to Jesus.* It changes my outlook dramatically, even if that person is engaged in something undesirable. It reminds me to be compassionate. I have to ask God to just squash Me because Me will rise up and do and say mean things. But if He is living bigger in me than Me, then nothing comes more naturally than Love.

I don't have a master's degree in theology, so I could be very wrong here, but I think that the "Good News" is a lot more than just "You can get into heaven!" That's great, for sure, but I think that the good news is really that somehow God loves me, you, us and that He loves us *right now*, in the midst of our mistakes. It's the Good News for *today*, not just for eternity. Because frankly, if I were able to get into heaven, but God didn't love me and didn't want me there with Him, that wouldn't be very good news to me. So in our grand efforts at evangelism, I think we often miss the point. We're full of the ways and means of religion, empty of real Love. And to the rest of the world, all of our doctrine and our guidelines just sound like a clanging cymbal.

I've also started trying to pray that God would bring someone along my path who needs to be smiled at today or needs to be loved, and that He would show me how ... and that I will do it. Sometimes He does it, and I shy away from loving them. I don't let them merge in traffic. I pretend not to notice that they're trying to get my attention to ask me for spare change. I ease away from them slowly at the end of the show as they try to approach me. But I want to be better at it.

I might not be able to wrap my arms around God's neck, but I can take some Mountain Dew to Ron tonight. And somehow, in God's economy, that's kind of the same thing.

22

Leaking Light

THE BOOK OF MARK is like an action sequence from the television show *24*, full of sporadic scene changes, but with some additional weird chronology. It cracks me up.

Mark is like, *So this one time, we were going to the mountain, and Judas walks up and he says—no, wait, before Judas got there, I was talking with Peter, and you know ... hey, do you remember that time Peter walked on the water? Man, that was crazy! He just got out of the boat, and we were all freaking out! So anyway ... wait, where was I? Oh yeah, Judas! So Judas says to me ...*

Mark also talks a lot about the way that Jesus acted toward the world at large and the people who didn't believe in Him.

If the Bible weren't true, I think I would expect it to show off Jesus' relationships with important people, telling how He was best buddies with kings and principalities. That would be the standard way to make sure everyone is impressed with the made-up version of Jesus. But the interesting thing about the Truth is that Jesus spent so much time doing the exact opposite of that. He was shockingly attentive to the untouchables, the underbelly of society.

The entire business of relating to the world is wrapped up in confusing, indefinite answers. It's something I encounter regularly on the road (and throughout life, in general). I'm always left wondering if I've approached it the right way. I end up in long conversations after shows where people want to talk about relating to pop culture, about the Church's responsibility to meet people where they are, about being "light in the darkness." And I don't have answers.

Sometimes I have an opportunity to let Jesus shine a little bit of light through me to the people at the venue where I'm playing, and I love those moments when He shows up like that—this big, beautiful Thing in the smallness of a conversation. It rarely happens from the stage. It usually only happens in those conversations after shows. Touring has reminded me how relational God is, and how that plays out in all of my relationships, new and familiar.

Sometimes the people I meet on the road talk about changing the world on a giant scale, through the media. Usually the first outlet that comes to mind is whichever one they happen to adore. "I want to change the world through MTV," they'll say. "I want to be a light in the darkness that slowly but surely works its way into their world and changes their hearts." And I wonder if God would ever choose to work that way. I know He changes individual hearts, but I don't think MTV can become a Christian company any more than one of my songs can become Christian.

Let's imagine for a moment that the head of MTV Networks becomes a Christian. Let's imagine that he feels incredibly convicted about selling sex and sin to teenagers, about glorifying drug use and promiscuity and underage drinking. So he cleans up the entire act. *The Real World* only shows the wholesome moments, and the guys and girls live in different houses. *Laguna Beach* girls don't want to shove each other into the riptide. The annual spring break week is just taken off the air entirely.

What would happen is that no one would watch MTV anymore. Not even the Christians. Slowly but surely, MTV would fall into bankruptcy while some other network would rise up to fill the void. And that new network would become the next one to influence pop culture in the way that MTV currently does.

Sin sells. MTV and the rest of the mainstream media mass-produce it. It is what the world wants to buy, and if they don't find it on MTV, they will build it and consume it elsewhere. It's like we're trying to chip away at the tip of the iceberg without address-ing the real problem: we are desperate wrecks without Jesus. We want the world to have a form of morality, instead of recognizing that this is a broken world and that Jesus has already told us it's only going to get worse until He returns. What would really be great would be to show people how Jesus really does care about the details of their lives, but that seems to happen primarily on a relational, not corporate, level. This legitimate desire to "rescue MTV" (or whatever) seems like a subconscious, misguided attempt to make the world accept us.

I recognize that notion well, because it exists in me too. When I was in high school and college, there was an idea that we passed around a lot: "You can be cool *and* be a Christian! Christians are cool!" We set out to prove it to the people at our schools by having pizza parties and flashy PowerPoint presentations and a really good worship band that sounded like U2. And all the hot people went to our church, too. It made it fairly easy not to be ashamed of the

Gospel—not because of what Jesus did, but because we were *so freaking cool.*

It didn't work, though. The world didn't buy it. Our numbers grew, but it was mostly just because people were leaving other churches to come to ours. We weren't consistently drawing in people whose lives were changed by the Gospel. It was shallow and self-serving, and it wasn't at all what Jesus did.

When this started to prove pointless, we tried a new approach. Instead of "Check it out—Christians are cool," we began tackling it from the opposite angle, the "cool things are Christian" angle.

"Hey, you like Switchfoot? Guess what—they're Christians! Ha-ha! We tricked you! You like Christian music! See, we're cool! You should've known that already by our cool website!"

* * *

As the Church, we're missing a world of opportunity to love people who need loving when we only try to love the people who are already loved and adored by everyone else on the planet. And I know this, because I do it all the time.

I want the world to validate me so that I don't have to sacrifice my hip factor by being a Christian. But Jesus told us over and over again that the world would hate us. So if the world doesn't hate us, then either Jesus was a liar or something is terribly wrong with the way we live our lives.

From what I understand, we are supposed to be countercultural, not a subculture. We are supposed to be obviously different. No, I'm not saying we should start dressing poorly and acting dorky, but I personally wish that I were a lot less concerned with wanting to be identified with the cool kids. Sometimes I'm ashamed to tell people that my music is "like Sheryl Crow, if she loved Jesus," so

I just say, "It's kind of like Sheryl Crow." It's not about salvaging my artistic credibility—it's about me wanting the cool kids to love me. And that is ridiculously lame.

Jesus went to those people who others didn't care so much about. I don't notice Him ever trying to win over the powerhouses. In fact, the only time that I can remember Him talking with a potentially cool and influential person (prior to His trial) was when He talked with the rich young ruler. He presented the truth, and it was ugly: Leave everything—your status, your wealth, your cool-ness—and follow Me.

There's a whole world of lost people out there, and most of them aren't super cool by traditional standards. In fact, the super-cool ones are the ones who are less likely to feel the pressing need to be rescued, because life can be so comfortable when you're hot, rich, and happy. But the broken, the bruised, the discarded peo-ple—they're aching for hope, and they'll openly admit it. I meet them at every show, and I'm always tempted to ignore them, which tells me that I desperately need *not* to, because that's what *every-one* does to them. I have to fight with this part of myself a lot.

*   *   *

Last year I went to a massage therapist in Nashville after com-ing back from a three-week tour of the Northeast. My body ached from sleeping on random surfaces for weeks at a time, from the fifteen-hour drive home, from the sedentary lifestyle of sitting in my car all day long, and from not being able to find time to work out. I could not wait to lie down on the massage table and start the healing process.

"I'm Vickie, and I'll be your massage therapist today," she said as she lit the aromatherapy candles and turned on the instrumental music. "How are you feeling?"

She was a rail-thin woman in her late thirties, tall and dark, with a soothing voice. The room was dim, and there was a heating pad on the table. I almost fell asleep immediately.

"I'm exhausted, but in good spirits," I replied, trying to keep it brief but friendly. "How are you?"

This was the equivalent of asking Richard Nixon how the early '70s were.

Vickie spent the next hour telling me how she lost her job after 9/11 and had to move back in with her parents at the age of thirty-four, and how she started dating a guy who abused her physically, which prompted her to become bulimic and subsequently look into some New Age religions for healing. At one point—when she was telling me how her new boyfriend was cheating on her—she cried.

Allow me to remind you that I was a total stranger, lying nearly naked in a dark room, paying her large sums of money to help me relax. I was incredulous. At the end of the massage, she left while I got dressed, then returned to direct me out of the spa. And then—no joke—she asked me for a hug.

"I just feel a special connection with you, and I appreciate the fact that you were so attentive to my story," she said as she pulled me in for the hug.

"Nmm pmmbmm,*" I mumbled into her shoulder.

(*translation: "No problem.")

I immediately felt like a jerk, but that feeling wore off pretty quickly when I had to fork over my hard-earned $70 at the front desk.

Kemper called the next day, and I told him about what happened at the spa.

"So when are you going back to see her?" he asked.

"Riiiiiiight," I said, laughing.

"I'm serious," he replied. I wasn't detecting any of his usual sarcasm. "This woman is crying out to you for help, sharing her life with you," he said, "and you're worried about seventy bucks? Get over it!"

"Ummm ..."

"God dropped her right into your lap—this person who needs the very hope that you have—and you're trying to tell me that you're not going to go back? How dare you!"

Well, he had me there. Reluctantly, I went back the next month and tried to love her the way Jesus has loved me my whole ugly, broken life. Again, she talked the whole hour. Again, she told me that she didn't act this way with everyone, but that I was "special."

Lucky me, I thought.

After a few months, she left the spa to work somewhere else, and I didn't know where to find her anymore. But I hope that something got through, despite my reluctance. For a long time, I could not figure out why God kept putting these aching people in my life, over and over again. Now I am pretty sure it's because I have felt His love, and I'm not intended to keep that kind of thing to myself.

> *And all Your children will stretch out their hands*
> *And pick up the crippled man.*
> *Father, we will lead them home.*
> —LEELAND, "Tears of the Saints"

* * *

There are so many types of people I encounter as I travel. It's exciting, because I grew up in a fairly homogenous part of the country. Some of the categories that people fall into have a way of making Christians feel like we're entitled to dismiss them, instead of loving them as though they were Jesus Himself, like He said we should do.

During the past few years, I've acquired quite a number of gay friends. It's not something that is widely accepted in the South. I grew up around the attitude that this, perhaps, is the worst of all sins. Far worse than pride or gluttony or greed. As the Church, we tend not to want to have to love "those people." And they know it. They *know* that we don't love them. And it makes them hate the Church. They are mirroring our hatred.

What would happen if they felt loved instead? What would happen if they could hear something besides that clanging cymbal when we spoke? If His people loved them first, instead of pushing them away, they might be more drawn toward Jesus.

> *How strong this change of heart must be*
> *That one that Jesus once described*
> *Kindness to your enemy—*
> *Carry his pack an extra mile.*
> —DAVID WILCOX, "Fearless Love"

Some of my gay friends grew up in the Church, and they know that the Bible spells out homosexuality as something that is not what God intends for us, but they, like all of us, are still tempted to sin. My friend Damon is a non-practicing homosexual, and I respect him more for that than I respect my Christian friend who is living with his girlfriend. Because Damon has the temptation but doesn't act on it. That's a lot more than I can say for myself and my own particular weaknesses. So I told him that recently. "You know what?" I said. "I am the Michael Jordan of jealousy, and I practice it often. As far as that is concerned, I'm living in sin more than you are right now."

Damon said that the most compelling argument for Christianity is rooted more in the reality of Christ's love than in condemnation. He said that if the Christian community could learn to leak light into the broken world more often, the world would start to pay attention. "It doesn't mean you have to offer approval of their actions," he said. "Just offer *love* to them, as fellow human beings."

If other people are anything like me, they probably don't stop doing something just because they hear that it's wrong or even because they may fear the consequences of it. (After all, I'm the church kid who stole an entertainment center over the course of a year.) The only thing that will change someone's actions is a change of heart. I know that comparing myself to other musicians is wrong, and I know it can have some painful repercussions, but I still do it. Likewise, simply hearing that homosexuality is a sin and that STDs are spreading rapidly throughout the world at large (not just in the gay community) will not make those in the gay community fall in love with Jesus. The only way anyone will ever turn to Jesus is if he or she feels His love. And you and I, my friends, are supposed to be the conduits.

23

Faking Love

DANGER AND I HAD a long list of things we wanted to do when we were in Manhattan over the holidays. On our first day there we stopped at the Museum of Modern Art, but we didn't want to fork over the $30 each for admission (I was thinking about how I could buy that great purse at H&M for the same price, and he, I'm sure, was thinking of orphans or something), so we just browsed the gift shop. Then we walked across East Fifty-third Street and turned down Lexington Avenue, heading to the Fifty-first Street station.

The wind on the Avenues moves like a freight train down the length of the City, gaining momentum as it passes between the skyscrapers. Danger looked straight ahead, squinting, adjusting his wool collar to combat the wind a little bit. I, on the other hand, was something of an embarrassment to him with my blatant displays of affection for the City. Our disparate personalities had never been more obvious. I might as well have been wearing a giant Nikon around my neck or one of those green foam Statue of Liberty crowns that all the school kids wear after their field trips there.

I craned my neck to get a better look at the Chrysler Building, my all-time favorite structure. He said, "You really love architecture, don't you?"

That surprised me—he had recognized that about me in the few short months we'd known each other, while I'd never even noticed it about myself.

"I guess so," I replied, realizing it was probably true.

"You comment on things about these buildings that would never catch my eye," he said.

"The Chrysler Building doesn't strike me as something unnoticeable," I laughed. "But hey, whatever."

We walked another block to catch the subway downtown for dinner. As we stood on the platform, I could feel him looking over at me. I had been smiling pretty broadly, and he asked me why.

"Do you realize that we're *underneath the world*?" I said. "We're *in* the earth! I know it's practically the same thing as being in someone's basement, but it's got this different feeling to know that cars and buses and fifty levels of steel and glass and cubicles are just above my head while I shuttle through this crazy, intricate system of tunnels and tracks."

He sort of nodded and turned away. We caught the train, and he sat, eyes fixed forward, staring into nothing.

It's not that I've never been to Manhattan or ridden the subway before. It's just that Manhattan is to cities what Texas is to states, and my love for it increases exponentially every time I'm there. That love is obvious to everyone because I can't suppress it. The thought entered my head that it might be annoying to him, but he saved me from the question when he said, "I think it's great that you're too busy having fun to waste time caring if other people notice or not."

Good, I thought. Because enthusiasm atrophies when it's stifled. Who wants to hide love?

> *I tell everyone I smile just because*
> *I've got a city love.*
> —JOHN MAYER, "City Love"

* * *

A few days later, I met up with Jane in Little Italy, and we talked until the early morning. We had both grown up in Christian families, and we talked about the "sorting time" that happens when you leave home for the first time and are no longer tied to tradition, when you are free to make your own decisions about what you believe. When college came and we entered our "sorting time," we both wound up on the "believers in Christ" side of things.

We wondered what it must be like for people who only know the rote practice of religion, who have grown up being taught a mathematical brand of faith. That road must be tough. It is futile to try to teach someone how to love something, pointless to merely convince them that they should.

I thought of Danger and the City, and I imagined saying to him, "When we get to the subway, smile and act giddy. And when we are outside, stare in awe at the buildings. This is what you do when you love the City." That would be an absurd waste of time, and it's not really teaching him how to be a lover of the City; it's merely teaching him how to emulate a lover, how to give lip service to real joy. Sometimes phony love is believable to the untrained eye, but it's still false.

This, to me, would be the equivalent of saying, "When you become a Christian, don't dance, don't drink, and don't have premarital sex. This is how you act when you love Jesus." Legalism seems like an attempt to showcase the effects of love, apart from the Object of love. I'd grown up around all those rules and regulations, and I know that they are probably a good idea for kids, but when you're an adult and you're making your own decisions, living by rules pales in comparison to loving something in a way that shows the change in you. I'm as guilty as the next of putting pale deeds on display, like some kind of membership card. Admittedly, I've been rebellious in some of my efforts to break free from that "membership card" mentality. But God is efficient: He didn't waste my wanderings. He used them to teach me more about what love *really* looks like.

* * *

I told Jane about my friend Emily and the day she blindsided me with the truth.

When I was a freshman in college, Emily called me and said, "Are you busy right now? Can I come over?"

"Sure. What's up?"

"I'll tell you when I get there," she said, and then she hung up immediately.

When we sat down in my living room, her opening line stunned me. "I need to tell you something: I'm not going to heaven when I die," she said.

"What are you talking about?" I asked, shocked. "I've been on missions trips with you! I've seen you tell *other* people about Jesus!"

She began to explain, in a patient, matter-of-fact tone: "Look, I know that God exists and that He loves me and that Jesus died on the cross for my sins. I know that He rose from the dead on the third day, and I know that His death is the only thing that makes a way for me to go to heaven. I know that I can't earn my salvation by being a good person. I know that the Bible is true, cover to cover ... *I just don't care.* It doesn't make a difference in my life."

The book of Romans talks about how everybody knows the Truth deep down, but that most people choose to suppress it in their hearts. That was the first time I'd ever met someone who openly admitted it. I struggled with her words for a long time. How could she know the Truth so fully and not respond to it?

She quoted Bible verses to me as she spoke. She talked about how the Bible says we must believe the Truth about Jesus in our *hearts.* She said that she believed it in her head, but not in her heart. She said, stoically, that she could not get that information to make the transfer that would change everything. I ached for her, but she seemed resolved not to believe.

I have no idea what makes the difference between Emily and me. It baffles me. But it also answers a lot of questions that I have about the world at large. It reminds me that God said He has given each of us a bit of faith for which we are responsible. Some of us respond and some of us don't, but we're all given the chance.

"Are you still going to call yourself a Christian?" I asked.

"Probably. It seems like the best description for the background that I come from," she said. "It's just a social identity thing, and that's the label that seems to fit the best, based on my heritage."

Emily effectively disappeared after that. She stopped showing up at church. She started drinking way too much and sleeping around, which were things she never did before. I think she felt like it was pointless to try to live a moral life when she wasn't attaching those morals to any kind of faith. I still struggle with the way she wanted to keep the moniker, but I know that I misrepresent Christ in so many ways too.

My heart broke for her. But at the same time, I respected her willingness to acknowledge the truth of her situation. It would've been easy to just keep pretending, to keep faking love.

* * *

I thought about my childhood and my parents. I remembered the way they lived their lives and how their actions always seemed motivated by love, not by fear or even by habit. It always seemed *real* with them. They had a faith that was, in the most literal sense of the word, unwavering. I saw them risk and hope and wait and grow. Jane and I talked a little longer, tossing around the question of what it takes to turn someone into an authentic lover of Christ like that.

I've loved two men in my life—Antonio and Harry—and I fell for both of them by being around them more and more, by finding out the beautiful things about them. I think that has also played a big part in the way I feel about Jesus. As I get to know more about Him, learn to pray about things that aren't purely selfish, spend more time with Him in a one-on-one relationship, I see how beautiful He is and feel His love for me, and I become smitten.

I think there's another piece to that puzzle too—a piece that has to do with community, with the family of Christ at large. One of the best ways for someone to fall in love with something, as author Don Miller said, is to see someone else love it firsthand.

When my parents lived their faith daily, I witnessed the difference it made. It loudly proclaimed, "Pay attention. This is no imposter." The difference that He made in them is what has made the difference in me. I saw true love, not feigned love. When I felt Jesus tugging at me, and I remembered the way my parents loved Him, it started to make me love Him too.

Love, I believe, is communicable.

* * *

After dinner, Danger and I went back to the subway to head to Central Park. From the corner of my eye, I saw him smiling broadly, and I turned to face him and ask him why. His eyes got wider, and he whispered, "Underneath the world!"

24

Doing the Retrospective Math

ON OUR LAST NIGHT IN THE CITY over the holidays, Danger and I had free tickets to a comedy club. We sat in the tiny room, smashed side by side with strangers, at a small table in the back corner. I have never laughed so hard in my life. After we left, we wrapped ourselves in coats and scarves and caught the subway at the Eighty-sixth Street station to ride down to Twenty-third. When we got off the train, we walked through the streets for a long time without saying a word—the Communist and the NRA member, walking arm in arm in satisfied silence.

He was supposed to catch the eleven o'clock train back to New Jersey, and I was going to the West Village to stay with a friend in the City that night. When we got to Penn Station, he said he wanted to wait and take the last train of the night. So we kept walking around in silence, just to be around each other for a little longer, going nowhere in particular. It struck me that it was a metaphor for our entire relationship.

I thought about everything that had happened since we'd met. Being with him gave me the same feeling I get when I fly over a familiar city—technically I'm there, but not really. I can't touch anything there. I can't visit my friends who live there. I can't connect. I can only stare at it longingly as I move on.

We were on Thirty-ninth Street when he spoke again.

"Am I boring you?" he asked.

"No, not at all," I told him.

"Are you having a good time?" he asked in a melancholy tone.

"Yes," I whispered sadly, without meeting his eyes.

"Good."

I looked at him, and he offered a painful smile and said something about how he just wanted to be in that moment, not to have to say anything but just to be there. So we were. He pointed to some concrete steps outside an old theater. We sat there and continued our silence.

A man who was walking past us stopped suddenly and said, "You two are such a beautiful couple!"

My face flushed with embarrassment, and I waited for Danger to respond so that I wouldn't have to do it. I knew I would've chosen the wrong words. "Thanks," he said in his uncertain voice.

The man stood there smiling at us for what felt like an eternity, but what probably amounted to three seconds. Then he said, "Well, have a good night," and walked away.

Danger and I sat there uncomfortably, because we *weren't* a couple—we were just two friends, saying goodbye in some sort of silent language. A few minutes later, he looked at me and gave me that look again—the one where his mouth was trying to smile but his eyes weren't in on the plan.

"This is it, isn't it?" he asked.

I inhaled and paused. "Yes," I said quietly, resigned.

We both just nodded and looked away. Then we stood and walked the last block to the train station, said our goodbyes ... and I knew I would never see him again.

* * *

Ten months later, I was sitting in a green room in Houston getting ready to go on stage, when my phone flashed: "Danger Calling." I was minutes from showtime, but I answered nervously.

"*Danger?*"

He was calling to tell me that he would be going home in twelve hours. From the tone of his voice, I knew that "home" meant Bolivia.

* * *

I think of that night a lot—the one in the mountains when we were lying on a blanket under the stars, freezing and talking about books and our pasts and our dreams. That is how I like to remember him.

I had to wonder, though, why God put this incredible man in my life—who loved Jesus, who was brilliant and kind, and who treated me like I was made of glass—if I wasn't supposed to be with him. It was spiritually frustrating because I wanted it to make sense.

Danger came along in the midst of my being in love with Harry—right when my heart was being destroyed. Sometimes I wonder if God brought him along just to show me that there are beautiful things in the world that will *not* destroy me. When I look at our relationship, I see how pure and amazing it was—but I think that maybe we were pieces from two different puzzles that just happened to fit together.

May you dream you are dreaming in a warm, soft bed
And may the voices inside you that fill you with dread
Make the sounds of thousands of angels instead
Tonight, where you might be laying your head.
—PATTY GRIFFIN, "Nobody's Cryin'"

* * *

I read something once that said we are like flies on the ceiling of the Sistine Chapel—we can only see the muck beneath our feet. Only when we step back to the Artist's viewpoint can we see the beautiful picture He is painting.

That's one of my favorite things about God—that He is big enough to take the good, the bad, and the ugly, and work them all together like some big masterpiece for my good and for His glory. It's like what the Bible says in Romans 8:28: "We know that God causes all things to work together for good to those who love God, to those who are called according to His purpose" (NASB). I've been learning that these strange, unexpected things that happen might not always *feel* like blessings, but the truth is that He is always only good. Even when I don't understand Him.

I think there are probably times when God prefers to be shrouded in mystery, and times when He wants us to see how His goodness is knit so tightly with His sovereignty. I'm not trying to solve His mystery by unraveling all these pieces of my story—I just don't want to miss anything that He might *want* me to see, because usually, when I *do* see it, it makes me love and trust Him more. It's like when David was going through some hard times in the Psalms, and he felt like God wasn't doing much of anything favorable. So he said that he would recount God's wonderful deeds of the past, and that helped him get through it. He knew God was with him.

We don't have much choice but to play life as it's handed to us and to trust God for the outcome. So far, I've seen Him walk me through frustrating, lonely times into amazing places of peace and joy and hope—to the seemingly unattainable dream that I was never qualified to live. I've felt Him pulling me with strong arms out of the sins that I adored, just because He loves me. It's the only way I ever learned how to start answering that question of whether or not I would love Him back. It reminds me of the line in the Caedmon's Call song "Lead of Love" that says, "I had to walk the rocks to see the mountain view."

All of my experiences recounted here have snowballed, building on top of each other, to make up the story of my life. And when I look at the story—from my unmet dreams of Harvard to Antonio's declaration of singleness to my desperate attempts to leave music— I can see His goodness in every scenario. As for the future, will I live in Manhattan? Will I marry or live alone? I don't know. But I can't wait to see what He will write for me next.

Here's to hindsight.

"Here's to Hindsight"
—TARA LEIGH COBBLE

Verse 1:

Here's to Antonio ... Broke my heart years ago
And in the space he left behind,
I picked up strings and wrote down lines
Here's to my guitar ... Like therapy for my heart
Drive through the night to scrape and sing,
Stage to stage, with faces in between ...

Chorus:

We'll raise our glasses to puzzle pieces
And the way they fit together that we never saw 'til now
Here's to questions that meet their answers
In the bright light of hindsight,
It will all come clear somehow

Verse 2:

Here's to my newfound friends ...
From out where the highway bends
They built a home in Tennessee
And left a little room for me
Here's to my patchwork world ...
Piece by piece, became the girl
Who lives just three miles from you,
The love that I could fall into ...

Bridge:

And all today's uncertainties, and all of my impatience
Will just be flecks of color
In the picture that He's painting

Epilogue
Letter to My Former Self

I mean this in the nicest way possible: you aren't quite as smart as you think you are. And you are still so much of a work in progress that I'm not sure when you'll be finished ... but it'll be a while. In the meantime, learn to enjoy changing and being corrected, because those are good things, and they will serve to shape you into the person you are going to be for the rest of your life.

First of all, you are not going to Harvard. Get over it. It's okay, though, because that will set you up for the ride of your life. Buckle up.

Someday soon, you'll meet a few incredible people who will start to paint pictures in your life that aren't too pretty. One of them will be a woman named Judy, and she'll tell you hard truths over long lunches. There'll be one lunch in particular (this will be at

Wendy's) where she will seem like the meanest woman alive. You will leave frustrated, but over time you will become more and more grateful for her words. Write down what she says and read it frequently. You will need to refer to it when you forget that she's right.

There will also be a woman named Debbie who will encourage you in ways you never imagined. And in case you don't know this yet, encouragement doesn't just take the form of sugary words that make you feel good about yourself. Sometimes it takes the form of a challenge ... it's truth dressed up as a dare. She'll challenge you to live out the wisdom that God has given. And when you fail, she will be there to love you and to pray for you. (P.S. Do not fall for her son, because he will marry someone else.)

Speaking of boys, you'll meet an amazing one someday. He will be a dashing Italian with a brain that won't quit. Welcome to love. When it's all said and done, you won't end up with him. But that's okay—go ahead and love him anyway. He will only draw you closer to Christ, with no steps backward on that path. When it ends, it will hurt terribly for a long, long time, and you will need distance from him in order to move on. Then one day (you won't even notice when this happens), the fog will lift. This will raise the bar of your expectations for relationships, and you'll be able to spot most of the imposters a mile away.

Start playing the guitar as soon as possible. When you do start, you'll think you're too clumsy, but trust me—just do it. And when you think it's time to invest in a good one, may I recommend a Taylor 810ce?

You'll record a few albums that will be progressively better, and you'll get to live your dream for at least a few years. It's not all that you think it is right now, but when it's good, it's even better than you hope.

Start paying close attention the moment you meet a man named Kemper. This is pivotal. He will know exactly how to encourage you with a strange brand of sarcastic wisdom. Take notes.

You will do things you swore you'd never do: You will move to Nashville. You will become a vegan. You will like a boy with blond hair.

Make sure to camp on the north rim of the Grand Canyon. See the Statue of Liberty. Get LASIK surgery as soon as possible. Vote. Sell the Saturn and buy a Camry. Tell your parents you love them every time you talk to them. Visit other countries. Speak to strangers. Don't spend too much time alone with your friends who are boys. Try to love people the way your mom has done her entire life. Never judge a person by your initial impression of him or her, because some of the closest friends you will ever have will be people who you initially did not like. Likewise, some of the people who you initially thought were incredible will prove you wrong and hurt you badly. But don't stop trusting in people. And remember that you suck sometimes, too.

When you're in your twenties, your friends will start to get married. You'll be mostly happy alone, but you will long for someone who will laugh with you and lead you and tell you when you're wrong—someone who will beckon you to walk with him to the feet of Jesus, who will challenge the way you think about a lot of things, who will patiently help you to be better. To a large degree, you will find this in your closest girlfriends. And I can't emphasize this enough: never underestimate the importance of solid, godly community. It's worth moving for.

Speaking of, you will move to New York City someday. You'll be confused about the decision for a long time, until one day, as you're walking down Broadway and praying about whether or not to relocate, you'll see the words "Move Up" written in chalk on the very section of sidewalk beneath your feet. Try to find an apartment near a subway line (maybe even in Greenwich Village) so that you don't have to walk very far—this will be important during the winters, when the air is so cold it freezes your plasma. While you're there, you will be the poorest you've ever been in your life, but also the happiest.

This is not very important in the grand scheme of things, but I think you should know that it is physically impossible for mascara to make your eyelashes longer. That's like saying paint makes a wall taller.

Words from Judy that you will wish you knew sooner: never advise a man on anything, even the quickest route to the store, unless he asks. And if he does ask, speak with exhaustive caution.

Words from your dad that you will never forget: a battleship starts to go in the opposite direction simply by moving off course one degree at a time—so be careful of your actions today, because they are slowly writing the story of your tomorrows.

Take your words and actions very seriously (because you are the world's picture of Jesus), but take yourself very lightly. Never write letters to yourself or refer to yourself in the second person, because that's pretentious and people will laugh at you.

And one more thing: sushi isn't so bad after all. Give it a shot.

About the Author

TARA LEIGH COBBLE is a singer/songwriter who has record-
ed and released five albums, including her latest *Here's to Hindsight*. When she isn't playing concerts, she is a freelance writer and
a frequent speaker on a variety of topics for college, young adults,
singles, youth, and women's groups. Her writings have appeared
in *RELEVANT*, *Radiant*, and *RELEVANT Leader* magazines. She
lives in New York City, where she has no children, pets, plants, or
anything else that might die if she forgets to feed it.

To book Tara Leigh Cobble for a concert or speaking
engagement, contact Shrinking Music:
615-504-1549
booking@taraleighcobble.com

www.taraleighcobble.com
www.herestohindsight.com
www.myspace.com/taraleighcobble
www.myspace.com/herestohindsight